WHAT DOES
CHINA THINK?

MARK LEONARD

WHAT DOES
CHINA THINK?

PUBLICAFFAIRS
A Member of the Perseus Books Group

Library of Congress Control Number: 2008921270
ISBN: 978-1-58648-484-2

10 9 8 7 6 5 4 3 2 1

To Gabrielle

CONTENTS

ACKNOWLEDGEMENTS

After September 11th there was a heated debate about Europe's relationship with America. The Western world appeared to split into two competing blocs representing different models of world order: Americans from Mars; and Europeans from Venus. The United States, on the one hand, wanted to use its military might to remain the only superpower – building a liberal world order in its own image. The European Union, on the other hand, represented a system where security was guaranteed through political and economic interdependence, and disputes were settled through law rather than power.

It was this intellectual ruckus that inspired me to write my first book, *Why Europe Will Run the 21st Century*, which argued that the birth of the European model is an achievement of historical significance. I set out a vision – which I still believe in – of how Europe's model could become the most influential system in the world by the end of the century. Today, that split between Europe and America has been complicated by a starker ideological competition that pits *both* the EU and the US against alternative systems which hail from beyond the west. The Russian credo of 'Sovereign Democracy' and the Islamist dream of theocratic rule already pose a serious challenge, even if they may yet turn out to be temporary phenomena. But it is China, with its vast size, its economic dynamism, and the political skill of its leaders that is the most serious contender for global leadership in the long term.

Although dozens of books have been published about China's

1

rise, most authors treat it as an economic, political or military bloc rather than seeing it as a powerhouse of ideas that could influence our world. They have little to say about China's intellectual debates, or the ideological competition they might pose to the European and American world-views. My work tries to make sense of these ideas which European policymakers will need to understand if they want to successfully promote their own world-view.

This book, like my previous one on Europe, would not have come into being without the support of my agents Maggie Pearlstine and Jamie Crawford. But the book's completion is a result of the vision of my editor at Fourth Estate Mitzi Angel. Together with her talented colleague Robin Harvie, she has been my creative super-ego, driving me to write and to do better with her unusual mix of intellectual brilliance, sensitivity, and patience.

I am indebted to many Chinese thinkers, writers and officials who have taken the time to talk to me, to share their writings, and debate ideas with me on my trips to China. They are too numerous to mention, so I will single out a few who have been especially helpful: Chu Shulong, Cui Zhiyuan, Fan Gang, Fang Ning, Feng Zhongping, Gan Yang, Han Deqiang, He Zengke, HS Liu, Hu Angang, Huang Ping, Jiang Xiaojuan, Jin Canrong, Kang Shaobang, Lai Hairong, Li Daokui, Li Dianxun, Li Jinghua, Li Junru, Liu Jianfei, Ma Zhengang, Pan Wei, Pan Yue, Pang Zhongying, Qin Gang, Qin Hui, Qin Yaqing, Ruan Zongze, Shen Dingli, Shen Dong, Shi Yinhong, Song Xinning, Wang Hui, Wang Jisi, Wang Shaoguang, Wang Xiaodong, Wang Yiwei, Wang Yizhou, Wu Baiyi, Wu Jianmin, Xianglin Xu, Yan Xuetong, Yang Jemian, Yang Yao, Yu Jiafu, Yu Keping, Yu Yongding, Zha Daojiong, Zhang Weiying, Zhao TingYang, Zheng Bijian, Zhou Hong. I am particularly grateful to my friends at the Chinese Academy of Social Sciences for hosting me on multiple trips to Beijing, and for welcoming me as a visiting scholar in the summer of 2006.

I have been inspired by the work and assistance of a number of veteran China-watchers including William Ehrmann, Aaron Friedberg, Joseph Fewsmith, Christopher Hum, Rod Macfarquhar, Lolita and Mattei Mihalca, James Miles, Eberhard Sandschneider, Ian Seckington, and David Shambaugh. Rem Koolhaas opened my eyes to a different China. Volker Stanzel has been a constant guide, a generous host and a wise counsel – convening fascinating lunches and dinners and frequently helping me make sense of my findings on trips around the country. Robert Kagan and Gary Schmitt were fascinating companions and sparring partners on trips to Beijing, Shanghai and Taipei. At various times and in their various ways, friends have given me critical support or ideas in ways they may not even be aware of. I should thank in particular Rob Blackhurst, Richard Gowan, Toby Green, Phoebe Griffith, Sunder Katwala, Adam Lury, Geoff Mulgan, and Shauna McAllister.

Much of the research for this book was conducted when I was working at the Centre for European Reform. I am grateful to Charles Grant, an intellectual companion and an exemplary employer for supporting this book from the outset, accompanying me on several trips to China and allowing me to take a sabbatical to work on the book. The German Marshall Fund paid for and organized several trips to China, and funded my work at CER. Its president, Craig Kennedy – a mentor and consiglieri – immediately understood the potential of the project, and once again gave me the personal and professional backing to see it through. At the Open Society Institute, three inspirational figures – Mabel van Oranje, Aryeh Neier, and George Soros – have been generous with support and advice, and patiently allowed me to finish a draft of the book before setting up the European Council on Foreign Relations. At the European Council on Foreign Relations, François Godement and John Fox, two brilliant observers of Chinese foreign policy, both read the text and gave me valuable feedback;

while my PA Katherine Parkes was a tower of strength throughout our eventful launch period.

Zhang Feng was a model research assistant and sounding board, ferreting out material, translating multiple articles and books, and keeping me in touch with the hottest ideas in Chinese academia and policy circles.

Three people introduced me to China on my very first trip and have been my guides ever since. Joshua Ramo, a soul-mate and inspiration, first got me hooked when he allowed me to publish his brilliant paper on the 'Beijing Consensus' when I was running the Foreign Policy Centre. He has been incredibly generous with his precious time, contacts, and ideas. Poppy Sebag-Montefiore made China trips fun as well as interesting. More than anyone else, she gave me an insight into everyday China, introducing me to her incredible friends, and letting me stay whenever I needed in her Beijing apartment. Andrew Small has been a true partner in crime, accompanying me to remote backwaters in the Chinese country-side, feeding me with reading materials on a bewildering array of topics, reading all my drafts, and helping me make sense of a whole new world.

My parents frequently put their own projects on hold to help me get through my latest crisis, humbling me with their generosity and intelligence. Their example makes everything seem possible, and their recognition makes it all worthwhile. My sister Miriam and her husband Phiroze have been there for me at all the crucial moments, giving me moral support, access to university archives and inspiring me with their own scholarship. But it is to my wife, Gabrielle, who lived on the frontline of this project for longer than either of us ever imagined, that this book is dedicated: If not for you my sky would fall, rain would gather too. Without your love I'd be nowhere at all, I'd be lost if not for you.

Mark Leonard, *November 2007*

INTRODUCTION

The Liberation of Thought

China's very existence creates a problem for Western accounts of world history. The Bible didn't say anything about China. Hegel saw world history starting with primitive China and ending in a crescendo of perfection with German civilization. Fukuyama's 'end of history' thesis simply replaces Germany with America. But suddenly the West has discovered that in the East there is this China: a large empire, with a long history and glorious past. A whole new world has emerged.

> Gan Yang, 'The Grand Three Traditions in the New Era:
> The Integration of the Three Traditions and the
> Re-emergence of the Chinese Civilization'

Very few things that happen during my lifetime will be remembered after I am dead. Even 9/11 or the Iraq War – events which transfixed us, took innocent lives and decided elections – will gradually fade until they become mere footnotes in the history books. But China's rise is different: it is the big story of our age and its after-effects could echo down generations to come. Like the rise and fall of Rome, the Ottoman Empire, the British Raj or the Soviet Union, it is the stuff from which grand narratives are wrought. For the first time since the end of the Cold War, a non-Western power is in the global premier league: China has joined the United States and Europe as a shaper of world order.

China's scale is mesmerizing; its vital statistics are almost impossible for us to grasp. With one in five of the world's population, China's entrance into the global market place has almost doubled the world's workforce. Already, half of the world's clothes and footwear have a 'Made in China' label in them, and China produces more computers than anywhere else in the world. China's voracious appetite for resources is gobbling up 40 per cent of the world's cement, 40 per cent of its coal, 30 per cent of its steel and 12 per cent of its energy. China has become so integrated into the global economy that its prospects have immediate effects on our everyday lives: simultaneously doubling the cost of petrol while halving the cost of our computers, keeping the US economy afloat but sinking the Italian footwear industry.

The speed at which this is happening is even more shocking. Building construction in Shanghai takes place at such a breakneck pace that the city's maps need to be rewritten every two weeks. A town the size of London shoots up in the Pearl River Delta every year. In the run-up to the Olympics, China is building enough new roads to go four times around the world. China has brought 300 million people from agricultural backwardness into modernity in just thirty years – a process of industrialization that took over 200 years in Europe. If current growth trends continue – which is admittedly a big 'if' – the People's Republic could overtake the USA to become the world's biggest economy well before 2050.

But this focus on scale, speed and measurable statistics is blinding us to a deeper question: will China's rise change the nature of our world? We are getting used to China's growing influence on the world economy – but could it also reshape our ideas about politics and power? China is the first country since the end of the Cold War with the ingenuity, scale and global exposure to shape the world in its image. Its gargantuan domestic problems are driving it to seek a new model of globalization. And its huge size means that other economies and nations connected to it – from America to Zimbabwe – will need to reformat their own systems to cope with China's new ideas about economic development, political reform and world order. China is starting to think for itself. And, because of its stunning economic record, people around the world are starting to listen, and copy the Chinese model.

This story of China's intellectual awakening is much less well documented than the now familiar tale of China's economic revival. Although we obsessively study the ideas of different factions in America's intellectual life – the Neo-Cons, the assertive realists, the religious right – how many of us can name more than a handful of contemporary Chinese writers or thinkers? Who knows what future they dream of for their country, or the world it is shaping? Europeans and Americans, in particular, are ill-equipped to answer these questions. Since the time when French and British missionaries first travelled to the East, the West has focused on what it wanted from China – and how to convert the Chinese to a Western way of life. People wrongly assumed that as China grew richer, it would also become more like us.

The accidental sinologist

China crept up on us slowly in the 1990s. For most of that decade, it was the preserve of regional specialists or fantasists from the business world who dreamt of making vast fortunes, but usually lost even more. However, at some indeterminate point around the turn of the millennium, China stopped being a subject for specialists. From my vantage point as director of a foreign policy think-tank in London, I remember noticing how – all of a sudden – almost every global challenge had acquired a Chinese dimension: from African development to the reform of the United Nations system, the Doha global trade talks to the Iranian nuclear programme, genocide in Darfur to oil prices in Venezuela. China was no longer a big country with which one could choose to enjoy trading or diplomatic relationships; instead it was starting to become part of the furniture of global politics, a universal factor with which we are forced to contend. In terms of political influence China had stopped being like other large developing countries such as India or Brazil. It was turning into something quite new: a miniature USA. I suddenly knew that without understanding China, it would be impossible to understand world politics.

I will never forget my first visit to the Chinese Academy of Social Sciences (CASS) in Beijing. I was welcomed by Wang Luolin, the academy's vice-president (whose grandfather had translated Marx's *Das Kapital* into Chinese), and Huang Ping (a former Red Guard who was then co-editor of the intellectual journal *Dushu*). Sitting in oversized armchairs – arranged in parallel against the wall in order to protect the backs of the hosts and guest of honour from enemy attacks – we sipped ceremonial tea and introduced ourselves. 'The Foreign Policy Centre,' I began, 'is four years old. We have around twenty staff, we publish twenty-five policy reports a year and host around fifty seminars.' Wang Luolin nodded politely and smiled before delivering his killer blow: 'CASS is the highest academic research organization in the fields of philosophy and social sciences. We have fifty research centres that cover 260 disciplines and sub-disciplines, and 4,000 full-time researchers.' As he said the words, I could feel myself shrink into the seams of my vast chair: Britain's entire think-tank community is numbered in the hundreds; Europe's in the low thousands; even the think-tank heaven of the USA cannot have more than 10,000. But here in China, a single institution – and there are another dozen or so other think-tanks in Beijing alone – had 4,000 researchers. I discovered later that even people at CASS think that many of these researchers are not up to scratch, but the raw figures were enough to intimidate me in that early meeting.

Wang Luolin's one-upmanship on size was just the beginning of a well-worn strategy designed to bewilder and co-opt outsiders. We spent many hours engaged in polite conversation without touching on the specifics of our co-operation. These elaborate courtship rituals, seemingly devoid of substance or direction, have been honed over centuries to nullify Western negotiating strategies, and bind foreigners into Chinese ways of doing things, creating webs based on personal contact rather than contractual obligations. At the beginning of the trip, I had hoped to get a quick introduction to China, learn the basics, and go home. But after spending what felt like weeks in these introductory meetings, sitting around sipping tea and exchanging pleasantries I ended up getting sucked in.

I had stumbled on a hidden world of intellectuals, think-tankers and activists who were thinking big thoughts. I soon realized that it would take more than a few visits to Beijing and Shanghai to grasp the scale and ambition of China's internal debates. My mind was made up – I wanted to devote the next few years of my life to understanding these radical developments; to document the living history that was unfolding before me. I became, so to speak, an accidental sinologist, visiting Beijing so frequently that it began to feel like a second home. And, with each visit, my entanglement with China's fate grew deeper. I became friendly with many of China's new thinkers and watched their theories develop over time, evolving in tandem with the breathtaking changes to their country. I saw them take Western ideas and adapt them into a new Chinese approach for dealing with the world – joining an intellectual journey that China began when it first became entangled with the West in the nineteenth century.

9

China's Ground Zero

The old Summer Palace in Beijing was as large as a city. People who saw it said it was more grandiose than the pyramids; more perfect than the Parthenon; and more transcendent than Notre-Dame. Even Victor Hugo, a man rarely stuck for words, struggled to capture its beauty: 'Build a dream with marble, jade, bronze and porcelain,' he said, 'cover it with precious stones, drape it with silk, make it here a sanctuary, there a harem ... gild it, paint it, have architects who are poets build the thousand and one dreams of the thousand and one nights, add gardens, basins, gushing water and foam, swans, ibis, peacocks, suppose in a word a sort of dazzling cavern of human fantasy with the face of a temple and palace, such was this building.'

But this edifice, which took 150 years to build, went up in a whiff of imperialist smoke when British and French troops stumbled upon it in 1860. All that is left today are a few desultory fragments and some cardboard scale models which signally fail to conjure up the palace's former glory. These dilapidated remains have been carefully preserved by successive Chinese governments. Like the scar of Ground Zero in New York City, they play a defining role in the Chinese psyche – arguably as great as any building that is still standing. The memory of the Summer Palace, 'Yuanmingyuan' as it is known in Chinese, acts as an open wound that can be salted whenever citizens need to be mobilized, or reminded of how the Communist Party saved China from foreign defeat. Yuanmingyuan is a physical embodiment of the 'century of humiliation' which ran from China's defeat in the Opium Wars of 1840, through the loss of Taiwan, the various Japanese invasions and the civil war right until the Communist Revolution of 1949.

For some intellectuals, the remains of Yuanmingyuan also

tell another story about modern China. This story is not about the damage which colonial powers have done to China, but of the destruction which the Chinese have inflicted upon themselves by importing – and misapplying – foreign ideas. In July 2006, Zhang Guangtian, an avant-garde theatre director, staged a controversial play, called *Yuanmingyuan*, that dramatized the relentless quest to modernize China by importing ideas from abroad, a history that has seen the country leap from one totalizing philosophy to another. Zhang Guangtian's play challenged his compatriots with a heretical question: who really destroyed Yuanmingyuan? Taking the spotlight off the imperial powers, he showed how the Chinese people themselves have been complicit in the despoiling of this national icon which he treats as a metaphor for their dreams and ideals.

The story begins in 1860 with a group of peasants who lounge around, complaining bitterly about the Chinese emperor's neglect of ordinary people. When a British soldier arrives on the stage, the peasants encourage him to attack the imperial palace so that they themselves can loot its remains. The same three actors then metamorphose into idealistic students – part of the 4 May 'Science and Democracy' Movement of 1919 – who desecrate the 'feudal' ruins to show their commitment to Western modernity. In the next scene the same actors return as Red Guards from the Cultural Revolution, turning the ruins into a rice paddy to show off their revolutionary fervour. The guards, in turn, become bureaucrats from the 1980s who line their pockets by converting the holy site into an amusement park. The action then shifts to 2005 when the same actors play local officials who line the lakes of Yuanmingyuan with plastic sheets in a bid to save water, causing such outrage that they provoke the country's first ever public environmental hearing. The second part of Zhang Guangtian's play is an unflinching exposé of the problems caused by China's recent embrace of the market:

environmental pollution, official corruption, the growing gap between rich and poor, the appalling conditions of China's mines. The play confronts the audience with the need to take responsibility for China's problems rather than assigning blame on foreign invaders. The playwright's message is subtle: it is not a plea to shut China off from the world, but a call to his fellow citizens to forge their own path into the future, rather than blindly embracing Western goods and ideas. His play gives dramatic form to the question that is mobilizing his native country: what does China need to do to take control of its own destiny?

Under the shadow of globalization

A growing body of Chinese thinkers believe that since their country crawled out of the chaos of the Cultural Revolution, it has simply replaced the shadow of Maoism with another fundamentalist philosophy: the cult of the United States of America. They complain that when Deng Xiaoping opened China's doors to the world, it was the USA that burst in. Its market philosophy set the rules for economic development. Its demands for democracy set the standards for political reform. And its foreign policy defined what was acceptable and unacceptable on the world stage. The USA has taken on the role of an all-powerful god whose moods define the weather. In the same way that Chinese peasants of old lived in constant fear of divine retribution, China's most pressing goal has been to avoid the wrath of the hegemon, crafting a foreign policy that hides China's 'brightness' with humble behaviour, while making ritual sacrifices on issues ranging from North Korea to Sudan in order to satisfy US demands.

For good and for ill, modernization became synonymous with Americanization in the 1980s and 1990s. At a superficial level,

Communist China shed its red skin, and grew a new one branded with the symbols of mass consumerism – Starbucks penetrated the walls of the Forbidden City, McDonald's and KFC signs lit up the high streets and malls of urban China, and kids learnt to cuss each other with Hollywood-inspired jibes: 'get real!' As the political scientist Yu Keping argues, 'The American dream is the highest ideal for the young generation that grew up since the reforms. Everything in the USA, including American people, institutions, economy, culture and country, is so perfect that the American moon has become more round than the one in China!'

At a deeper level, China was forced to accommodate itself to the rules of a globalized world shaped by American capital and American military power. In this era – christened the 'flat world' by the journalist Thomas Friedman – all nation states are losing control of their fates: pushed out of the economic sphere by privatization, out of the political sphere by a 'Third Wave' of democratization, and out of the foreign policy realm by the stateless forces of capital, terrorism and trade. Many Chinese thinkers worry that by embracing the economic benefits of globalization, China risks being 'flattened' by an accompanying American political ideology.

Wang Xiaodong, one of a new breed of Chinese nationalists, argues that the embrace of American ideas springs from a kind of self-hatred. According to him, many Beijing intellectuals in the 1980s saw the Chinese people as an inferior nation with an inferior history: 'In my opinion, this is not very different from Hitler's racism,' he claims, 'the only difference between them [i.e. Chinese intellectuals] and Hitler was that they [i.e. the Chinese] directed this [hatred] against their own race. This is why I coined the term "reverse racism".' Although Wang Xiaodong's analogy seems extreme and misplaced to many Chinese as well as Western ears, his arguments are symptomatic of a pervasive sense of intellectual insecurity that has driven China's swings from one extreme ideology to the next.

Liberation

In 1993, Cui Zhiyuan, a Tsinghua University professor who was then teaching at Massachusetts Institute of Technology, wrote a seminal article calling for a new 'Liberation of Thought', arguing that after freeing themselves from orthodox Marxism, Chinese intellectuals should liberate themselves from their unquestioning admiration of Western capitalism. His goal was to break the boom and bust cycle that saw China embrace a new ideology every generation, and to encourage Chinese people to think for themselves. Rather than accepting the mantra that 'there is no alternative' to the neo-liberal agenda, he argued that China should draw on many sources to develop a new way, or as he put it an 'alternative modernity'.

His call initially fell on deaf ears. China was still reeling from the Tiananmen massacre. Most of its intellectuals were cowed by the government's violent response to the protests, co-opted by the Communist Party or living in exile. Party leaders were restarting their economic reforms. And the rest of the elite were too busy making money. But Cui Zhiyuan's ideas are having an impact today, as China's economic growth leads to a new self-confidence.

Even the nationalist Wang Xiaodong acknowledges that his country is outgrowing 'reverse-racism'. In a recent talk, he cited the words of a well-known entrepreneur to make the point: 'In the 1980s I went out of China for the first time, to Singapore ... I was shocked by the culture, the technological progress, the urban splendour, the vibrancy of life. Our delegation dreamt "Could our country have a city like Singapore in fifty years time?" We were not hopeful. History has proven us wrong. It took just twenty-five years. Last year I went to Singapore, and in my view, it cannot compete with our Shenzhen, Dalian, Shanghai and Beijing.'

The self-confidence that comes from China's economic miracle has – paradoxically – freed some of China's thinkers to question the central tenets of the market revolution that produced it. Now that Chinese thinkers take their country's giddy growth rates for granted, they are asking if the ideology of the 1980s and 1990s is really delivering all that it promised. Deng Xiaoping's commitment to economic development, above all else, is being attacked by those who want to reduce inequality and stop the pillage of China's environment. In the realm of political reform, some Chinese intellectuals are increasingly questioning whether liberal democracy is the right model for China in the long term. And in the realm of foreign policy, they are challenging the notion that nation states need to be marginalized by the stateless forces of globalization.

The intellectual emancipation that Cui Zhiyuan invoked is finally coming. In the same way that Europeans during the Enlightenment proclaimed that 'God is dead' and sought to craft a world in man's image, Chinese intellectuals are today proclaiming their independence from foreign models and plotting the future on their own terms. The quest, according to the political scientist Gan Yang, is to draw on China's historical experiences and create a new idea of modernity – rather than importing theories wholesale from abroad. He says:

> Today we can see in China three traditions. One is the tradition forged during the twenty-eight years of the reform era ... of 'the market at the centre' including a lot of concepts like freedom and rights. Another tradition was formed in the Mao Zedong era. Its main characteristics are striving for equality and justice. The last tradition was formed during the thousands of years of Chinese civilization, traditionally

15

referred to as Confucian culture. In the past we have often behaved as if these three traditions were in conflict with each other. But they are not.

This is not the first time that Chinese have sought to combine foreign know-how with national identity. Confucian reformers in the nineteenth century strove to bolster the imperial system by using foreign 'functional knowledge' (*yong*) to preserve Chinese 'essence' (*ti*). And Deng Xiaoping labelled his market reforms 'socialism with Chinese characteristics'. But where earlier generations started from a position of debilitating weakness, today's reformers are coming to terms with China's growing strength. And, what is more, this attempt is being bolstered by an intellectual debate raging beyond the halls of power.

The intellectual as king

This book is about the development of a new Chinese world-view. It shows how China's quest for intellectual autonomy will act as the foundation for a new model of globalization. It follows the attempts by Chinese thinkers to reconcile competing goals; exploring how they can get access to global markets while protecting China from the gales of creative destruction they could unleash in its political and economic system. It shows how China will come to challenge the flat world of American globalization with a 'Walled World' of China's own creation. Inspired by discussions with over 200 Chinese thinkers and officials over a period of three years, this book tries to chart China's recent intellectual emancipation from Western ideas on economics, politics and global power, casting light on how Beijing's new thinking could change the world order – thereby changing the West itself.

I do not purport to represent the multitude of views held by 1.4 billion people, or even the views of all Chinese intellectuals – many have been silenced by imprisonment, intimidation or exile. The thinkers represented in this volume are insiders. They have chosen to live in mainland China – learning to cope with the regime's regular spasms of control and loosening up – in their quest to push for change within the system. Even they have sometimes fallen foul of China's erratic censors. Several of the protagonists of this story have been stripped of important jobs in think-tanks and journals during the years that I have been writing this book – even as their ideas have received greater backing from the government. In spite of the ever-present threat of repression, incarcerations and censorship, intellectuals in China do count. Many of these thinkers have been called upon to brief presidents, prime ministers and senior party officials. In fact, they have more influence than their counterparts in many Western countries.

Paradoxically, the power of the Chinese intellectual is amplified by China's repressive political system where there are no opposition parties, no independent trade unions, no public disagreements between politicians, and a media that exists to underpin social harmony rather than promote political accountability. Intellectual debate, in this world, can become a surrogate for politics – if only because it is more personal, aggressive and emotive than anything that formal politics can muster. Intellectuals can articulate the concerns of broader social forces – workers, farmers, entrepreneurs – and push for change in their name. The Chinese like to argue about whether it is the intellectuals that influence decision-makers, or whether groups of decision-makers use pet intellectuals as informal mouthpieces to advance their own views. Either way, the debates between thinkers have become part of the political process, and are used to put ideas in play and expand the options available to Chinese decision-makers.

Although many scholars complain that Chinese intellectuals have lost their traditional role as the social conscience of the nation – and been co-opted by the government or drawn into arid specializations – the clashes between different factions, such as the 'New Left' and 'New Right', do capture real social divisions on the ground.

Thinkers like Wang Hui and Zhang Weiying, Yu Keping and Pan Wei, Zheng Bijian and Yan Xuetong are still practically unheard of outside of China. But we will soon find our world changed by their thinking. Each has won the ear of the government with plans for reform that will change the nature of China's economics, politics and foreign policy. They are engaged in an old-fashioned battle between Left and Right – about the size of the state, the shape of political reform and the nature of power. However, from their heated arguments a new philosophy is emerging, one that will have important implications for the world.

Of course, big decisions will always be taken by big leaders: China may not have embraced the market without Deng Xiaoping; Thatcherism would not have happened without Thatcher; the dissolution of the Soviet Union would not have happened without Gorbachev; and the Iraq War may not have been launched without George Bush. And yet it is impossible to understand the broad sweep of historical change without studying the intellectual movements that crystallize around certain ideas, on which the leaders can draw. Thatcher did not invent monetarism herself but drew on ideas which had been bubbling away for many years. George Bush was influenced by the ideas of Neo-Conservative intellectuals. Deng Xiaoping did not suddenly decide to open up China's market; he was influenced by perspectives developed by Chinese intellectuals who had been in contact with the West. And today there are new ideas bubbling up within China that could form the core of a new Chinese philosophy, the idea of a 'Walled World'.

CHAPTER ONE

Yellow River Capitalism

In the 1980s, we were all reformists. We criticized old-style Maoist goals and practices. We looked at our circumstances through the ideas of the West. What we got was naïve and abstract because we didn't really know what would happen to China once the market took off. We didn't know that the market would create rich and poor: we thought it would benefit everyone. And for a few years it did.

Gan Yang

It was the Cuban cigars that first caught my eye. Half a dozen boxes of Cohiba, Romeo y Julieta and Montecristo piled high on Zhang Weiying's desk in a haphazard monument to the economic opportunities of today's China. These almost Freudian status symbols – worth several times a Chinese peasant's annual income – are like pocket-sized pyramids, toiled over by workers for the rich to flaunt. Like the 300 skyscrapers of Shanghai or Beijing's new Olympic Stadium they testify to the nature of an economy where labour has become a commodity, and money is spent almost as quickly as it is earned.

But for Zhang Weiying they are also pocket-sized fragments of freedom; products of a parallel universe – a republic of the West – that has been built alongside the Communist state in China; one whose dynamism he hopes will gradually eclipse and replace the last vestiges of Maoism. Like other economic liberals – or members of the 'New Right' as their opponents call them – he thinks that the planned economy is the foundation of political despotism; that China's freedom will not come until the public sector is dismantled and sold off, and the state has shrivelled into a residual body designed primarily to protect property rights. Only then, according to the 'New Right', will a propertied class – a new civil society – be able to lay the foundations for democratic politics. The cigars, therefore, do not just show that getting rich is glorious, as symbols of private wealth they are milestones on the road to freedom.

Behind Zhang Weiying's desk a glass-fronted display case glistened with the trophies and baubles of a distinguished career: books he has written and edited, pictures of him with Nobel laureates and statesmen, degrees from leading universities, and an award for 'The Man of the Year in Chinese Economy' from Chinese Central Television (CCTV) in 2002. They all reinforce the point that Professor Zhang Weiying has made it; that he is one of the most famous economists in China. But life today is getting tougher for economists like Zhang Weiying. After thirty years of ruling the roost with imported ideas from the West, they can feel China turning against them. Opinion polls show that they are the least popular group in China – on a par with traffic wardens and used-car salesmen in the UK. Public anger is growing over the costs of reform, with protests by laid-off workers coming together with concern over illegal demolitions, corruption and unpaid wages and pensions. As a result, the ideas of the market are being challenged by a 'New Left' which advocates a gentler form of capitalism. A battle of ideas is raging which pits the state against the market; coasts against inland provinces; towns against the countryside; the rich against the poor.

The dictatorship of the economists

Success is all about timing, and Zhang Weiying's was perfect. He graduated with a degree in economics in 1982 – just as Deng Xiaoping's opening and reform process was gathering momentum. It is hard for Westerners, used to life in a fissiparous open society, to understand a purposeful state like Deng's China. Zhang Weiying frequently uses the word 'missionary' to describe the determination with which China pursued economic growth. In a similar way, Franz Kafka, the pre-eminent chronicler of life in the closed society, conjures up the singleness of purpose of the Chinese authorities in a different period in his essay on the Great Wall of China: 'Fifty years before the building was begun, throughout the whole area of China that was to be walled around, architecture, and masonry in particular, had been declared the most important branch of knowledge, all others being recognized only in so far as they had some connection with it.' When Zhang Weiying graduated in 1982, there was a new wall to build: China's market economy. The Communist Party had declared that economic growth was 'the central task', and suddenly everyone wanted to be an economist. 'Economics,' as Wang Hui puts it, 'acquired the force of an ethics.' As the economy grew, so did the influence and wealth of the economists. They populated government taskforces, wrote plans for privatization and filled the boards of the newly privatized companies (131 of 274 independent directors in today's listed enterprises are academic economists). They became the new high priests of China whose arguments increasingly trumped those of Maoist refuseniks (who were derisively known as *fanshipai* or 'whateverists' because they supported whatever policy decisions Chairman Mao made).

Deng Xiaoping's 'dictatorship of the economists', as disgruntled political scientists, philosophers and sociologists called it, produced startling results. An average of 9 per cent growth over three decades made China the world's third biggest economy by 2007. Three hundred million people rose from absolute poverty, while 200 million left their farms to work in industry. One hundred million joined the so-called middle class and 500,000 became millionaires. And a new generation of Chinese companies such as the computer giant Lenovo that bought IBM and the Nanjing car company that bought MG Rover entered the global corporate league.

Like Zhang Weiying's own success, China's economic miracle owed much to its timing. Unlike his Russian and Latin American counterparts who rapidly implemented measures to liberalize and privatize their economies – known as 'economic shock therapy' – the Chinese leader Deng Xiaoping did not have a mandate for radical reform. Many leading Communist Party officials such as Chen Yun, Li Xiannian and Deng Liqun were against market reforms. They continued to believe that China's problems could be fixed by modernizing the planned economy and making it 'more scientific', like its Soviet counterpart. Deng Xiaoping and his allies were, therefore, unable to set a blueprint or timetable for China's economic transformation. Instead, they opted famously to 'grope for stones to cross the river' – implementing incremental changes, one step at a time, without ever talking about the final destination. To his country's lasting benefit, Deng Xiaoping heeded Bertolt Brecht's advice that when there are obstacles, the shortest distance between two points can be a crooked line.

The village of zebras

Zhang Weiying has a favourite allegory to explain China's reforms. He tells a story about a village whose residents rely on horses to carry out all their chores. The village elders, who had tirelessly argued that their horses were better than the zebras used in a neighbouring village, would harangue anyone who questioned their claim. Over time, however, the elders realized that the neighbouring zebras were, in fact, superior to the idle and greedy horses which they had so actively promoted. So, after years of hailing the virtues of the horse, they decided to embrace the zebra. The only obstacle was converting the villagers who had been brainwashed over decades into worshipping the horse. The elders developed an ingenious plan. Every night, while the villagers slept, they painted black stripes on a few horses. When the villagers awoke – shocked at the presence of evil beasts in their midst – the leaders reassured them that the animals were not really zebras, just the same old horses adorned with a few harmless stripes. The villagers gradually became accustomed to the presence of the strangely decorated animals in their midst. After a long interval the village leaders began to replace the painted horses with real zebras. These prodigious animals transformed the village's fortunes, increasing productivity and creating wealth all around. Only many years later – long after all the horses had been replaced with zebras and the village had benefited from many years of prosperity – did the elders summon the citizenry to proclaim that their community was a village of zebras, and that zebras were good and horses bad.

Zhang Weiying's allegory is an explanation of his most famous idea, the theory of 'dual-track pricing' which he first put forward in 1984. He argued that 'dual-track pricing' would allow the government to move from an economy where prices were set by government officials to one where they were set by the market, without having to publicly abandon its commitment to socialism or run into the opposition of local governments with a vested interest in central planning. Under Zhang Weiying's approach some goods and services continued to be sold at state controlled prices while others were sold at market prices. Over time, the proportion of goods sold at market prices was steadily increased until by the early 1990s almost all products were sold at market prices. The 'dual-track' approach embodies the combination of pragmatism and incrementalism that has allowed China's reformers to work around obstacles rather than confronting them head on. Rather than closing down the old central planning system, they first created an alternative reality alongside it. And when things went well, they reformed the old system to give it the best features of the new reforms.

Pearl River Capitalism: from permanent revolution to permanent innovation

Zhang Weiying was not the only person to call for 'dual-track pricing', but he was the first to do it publicly. He was soon given a plum job working for the Commission for State Institutional Reform which he held down from 1984 until 1990. Zhang Weiying was part of a group of young officials who found ways of making market ideas palatable to the older Communist elite. Their goal was to paint as many zebras as possible – to create a parallel market in the shell of socialist China.

China's economic reforms had begun in the countryside with

the dissolution of the 'people's communes' and the end of collective farms in 1979. For over two decades before then, life in the countryside had been organized around collective 'work units' which lived together, worked together and ate together. The work unit was meant to replace the family as the primary unit of economic activity and social life. With the 'opening and reform era', these collective farms were closed down and replaced with smallholdings that were controlled by individual families who could decide what they wanted to grow, and more importantly kept the profits generated by their labour. This led to a huge surge in agricultural productivity which freed thousands of labourers from the fields. These workers were soon employed by a new crop of privately run factories – known as 'Town and Village Enterprises' – which sprang up all over the countryside. The wealth generated by China's rural revolution allowed the local governments to benefit from the revenue generated by private industry. But these primitive trysts with the market were not what excited Zhang Weiying and his colleagues. This was just the beginning.

In their quest for a new China they looked beyond the land-locked rural plains where economic reform had begun to the outward-facing coastal provinces of the east. At the beginning of the 1980s, Shenzhen was an unremarkable fishing village, providing a meagre living for its few thousand inhabitants. Over the next three decades it has become an emblem of the Chinese capitalism that Zhang Weiying and his colleagues were building. Because of its proximity to Hong Kong, Deng Xiaoping chose Shenzhen as the first 'Special Economic Zone', offering its leaders tax-breaks, freedom from government regulation and a licence to pioneer new market ideas. The architects of reform in Shenzhen were not interested in replicating the low-tech industrial revolution that had taken place in the countryside at the beginning of the era of 'opening and reform'. They wanted to build high-tech, capital intensive plants that could mass-produce the sort of high-value-added goods that could compete directly with the West. In order to get their hands on the technology and capital to turn their dreams into reality, the authorities set about attracting investment from abroad. Shenzhen alone succeeded in pulling in over $30 billion of foreign money to build factories and roads and develop its ports. The secret of Shenzhen's success was its reliance on exports, rather than domestic consumption to fuel its growth. The decision to open the 'Special Economic Zones' up to the outside world provided a booster for the development of a non-state sector because foreign companies would set up joint ventures and shareholding companies. As a result, by 1992 half of China's industrial output was generated by the non-state sector.

This pattern of building zones of radical experimentation to gradually produce more valuable goods and services was the key to China's success. It was very capital intensive, and needed to be financed by drawing on the country's massive savings and the revenues from exports rather than domestic consumption. It was based on the commodification of labour, as the coastal regions could suck in endless numbers of workers from the countryside in order to depress urban salaries. And it was laissez-faire – allowing wealth to trickle down from the rich to the poor organically rather than consciously redistributing it. Deng Xiaoping pointedly declared that 'some must get rich first', arguing that the different regions should 'eat in separate kitchens' rather than putting their resources into a 'common pot'. As a result, the reformers of the eastern provinces were allowed to cut free from the impoverished inland areas and steam ahead.

The take-off of the coastal regions seemed to back up the claims of generations of Chinese reformers that their country had been held back by the conservatism of its inland provinces, which prevented China from competing with maritime civilizations such as Britain, France, Japan and the USA which had embraced the market, trade and innovation. The reforms of the 1980s unleashed a process of social change that went far beyond economics. The Chinese called it a 'cultural fever'. It reached a cresc-endo in June 1988 with the showing of a six-part documentary called *River Elegy* in prime-time on the main state television channel. The series used the story of the Yellow River – often referred to as 'mother river' because it is considered to be the cradle of Chinese civilization – to launch a full-frontal attack on China's traditions.

Rather than accepting the romantic ideal of the Yellow River as the embodiment of Chinese greatness, the series presented it – with its countless victims from flooding and drought – as an enemy of the Chinese people; the ultimate symbol of their irrational, erratic and earth-oriented character. Each episode targeted a Chinese tradition that was holding the country back. For example, the Great Wall was treated as a symbol of meaningless isolation, while the Ming dynasty was attacked for its ban on maritime activity. The pungent style of the narrator drove this point home in the very first episode: 'There is a blind spot in our national psyche: it is a vague belief that all of the shame of the past century is the result of a break in our glorious history. Ever since 1840, there have been people who have used the splendours and greatness of the past to conceal the feebleness and backwardness of our present state ... Yet the fact remains, our civilization is moribund.' The narrators pleaded with China to break the bonds of traditional society that had prevented the country's modernization. China, they argued, must now turn away from the countryside, focusing not on the Yellow River, but rather on the blue world of the ocean and the world beyond. The final images of the series show the Yellow River dissolving into the powerful sea which symbolizes the might of the Western world which has embraced modernity. In China's universities and colleges, students spontaneously discussed and debated the issues raised in each episode of *River Elegy*. Five million copies of the script were sold as it became an instant best-seller. The reformist prime minister Zhao Ziyang arranged for the series to be re-aired on the main TV channel, Chinese Central Television.

Less than a year after the series was aired, the cultural fever took a decidedly political turn in the Tiananmen Square demonstrations of 1989. What began as a memorial march for the former Communist Party Secretary General Hu Yaobang on 15 April soon turned into a catch-all protest for political reform, workers' rights and an end to official corruption. This incredible display of people power that dominated the streets of Beijing for six weeks gave the world a glimpse of a democratic China until it was abruptly wiped out by soldiers and tanks on 4 June 1989. The crackdown was more than a human tragedy; it became a defining moment in China's political and economic development.

The two stories of Tiananmen

One of the students who was glued to the television during episodes of *River Elegy* was Wang Hui. He had been working on a PhD in Chinese literature when he joined the student demonstrations of 1989. Like most young intellectuals Wang Hui was a supporter of Deng Xiaoping's 'Open Door' policies and a believer in the potential of the market. But when Wang Hui left the demonstrations for the last time he embarked on an intellectual journey that would change his world-view: 'In the early morning of 4 June 1989, as I departed from Tiananmen Square in the company of the last group of my classmates, I felt nothing but anger and despair.' As the government rounded up and punished the organizers of the protest, Wang Hui took off to the mountains and spent two years in hiding, getting to know peasants and workers whose experiences made him doubt the justice of unregulated free markets, and convinced him that the state must play a role in preventing inequality.

Until 1989, reformist intellectuals had been united in a journey to the West, regarding political and economic liberalism as a seamless whole, one that would benefit all Chinese people. Their enemies were the 'conservatives' who supported the Maoist status quo. After the bloodshed the reformers split into two camps: a 'New Right', led by thinkers like Zhang Weiying, who see free markets as the most important goal and are willing to make an accommodation with political authoritarianism; and a 'New Left', about whom we will hear more later, led by scholars such as Wang Hui, who emphasize equality and political democracy at the expense of total market freedom.

These tensions had been inherent in the demonstrations themselves. In the West, we saw Tiananmen as a confrontation between a brutal, unreformed communist state and a group of students longing to be part of the capitalist world of liberal democracy. But, in an important essay on the meaning of 1989 (which he wrote retrospectively from exile in 1997), Wang Hui takes the spotlight off the intellectuals and students and puts it on a wider group of workers who came to the square with more concrete social and economic demands. Their involvement in the protests had been triggered by mounting discontent about the radical market reforms of 1988 which had set off rocketing inflation and inequality. These workers had no interest in being part of the West. In fact, what they wanted was price stability, social security and an end to corruption and speculation. Wang Hui sees their concerns as part of the global resistance to neoliberalism, comparing Tiananmen to the anti-globalization riots that erupted in Seattle and Genoa.

According to Wang Hui, there were two different agendas in the square: one group wanted social welfare and protection from the market; the other wanted democracy and protection from the leviathan Communist state. If the protesters had faced in two directions, so did the repression that followed it. According to Wang Hui, the crackdown not only silenced calls for democracy, it also ended public debate about inequality. Once the tanks had done their work, the process of marketization speeded up. The price reforms that had been called to a halt in the second half of 1988 were implemented in September 1989. After Deng Xiaoping reasserted himself over the conservatives in 1992 – using his famous 'Southern tour' of the coastal cities of Guangzhou and Shenzhen to restate the case for reform – many more changes followed. The corruption, the smuggling, the unfair distribution of assets, the influence of interest groups on public policy, the overdevelopment of real estate, the problems with the social welfare system and environmental concerns, which the protesters had complained about, got steadily worse.

However, the threat of further repression meant society's discontent was muted. As Wang Hui says: 'Just as people have forgotten the sound of social fragmentation echoing behind the excitement at Tiananmen, neither can people remember that the market era referred to today as "neo-liberalism" is hiding behind the political spectres of those on the square and has only in this way secured an exemption from social protest against it.' What he means is that the stodgy, bureaucratic face of the traditional Communist Party has masked the most extensive and ambitious process of marketization and privatization the world has ever seen. By referring to the market revolution as 'socialism with Chinese characteristics', the authorities were able to use quotes from Marx and Mao to repackage the ideas of Milton Friedman and Friedrich Hayek. For Wang Hui, the tanks that pulverized the hopeful intellectual flourishing of the 1980s were working on behalf of market fundamentalism rather than Maoism. Contrary to the view of the repression as a reassertion of Maoist ideology, the authoritarianism was acting to silence workers' anxieties about inequality. This is Wang Hui's version of the zebra story.

For Wang Hui, China's last fifteen years have felt like a hallucination:

> those who thought that the movement had speeded up the process of Chinese democratic development discovered that they had been abruptly dragged back into an era they thought was passing away – the old language, old patterns, old characters, old announcements, old faces that should have retired from the scene all took the stage once again. These old patterns created a hallucinatory effect, such that no one became conscious of the fact that the actual function of the repressive measures was precisely to re-establish the links among market mechanisms that had begun to fail.

On the surface it looked as though the old guard was emphasizing its Communist ways, but in reality market forces were being pushed through with unprecedented speed. This created an ironic situation where right-wing economists like Zhang Weiying – who like to talk about the withering of the state – have, in fact, been the biggest beneficiaries of one-party rule. The Communists have faithfully implemented his ideas for reform, while silencing critical voices on the Left.

Zhang Weiying was not immediately sure how things would pan out so he left Beijing for Oxford University to study for a PhD under the Nobel Prize-winning professor James Mirrlees. By the time he returned to China in 1994, the breakneck pace of reform had resumed. The size of the non-state sector had grown exponentially and China was already overcoming the international opprobrium which its brutal suppression of the demonstrations had provoked. Zhang Weiying immediately returned to the action, dividing his time between the business, academic and policy worlds. As well as sitting on a number of government task-forces, he runs the prestigious Guanghua School of Management at Beijing University, and advises a dozen of the biggest firms in China. Since 1995 he has been the most cited economist in Chinese economic journals.

Wang Hui and the left-wing reformers had a tougher time in the 1990s. Numbed by the ferocity of the assault on the protesters, disorientated by the bizarre alliance of convenience between the Communist Party and the new capitalist elite, and depressed by a growing body of thought that believed that history was coming to an inevitable end, he and his colleagues went underground. They fell back on the three weapons that James Joyce had advocated against repression: 'silence, exile, and cunning'.

The rise of China's 'New Left'

I met Wang Hui in 'Thinker's Café', a bright and airy retreat with comfy sofas and fresh espressos that sits on top of one of Beijing's largest bookshops. Within a stone's throw of three of the country's most prestigious universities – Tsinghua, Beida and Renmin – it reverberates to the sound of earnest intellectual chatter. Today's Wang Hui has overcome his despair. He has the guise of an archetypal public intellectual: a thin man with cropped hair, wearing a brown jacket and a black polo-neck sweater. He loves discussing abstract notions like 'enlightenment', 'teleology' and the meaning of 'modernity'. Neither his J.-P. Sartre chic nor his trendy theoretical discourse would be out of place on the Left Bank of Paris.

But Wang Hui has not lost his anger about China's condition. He has managed to stand aloof from the commercial mainstream. Because he has not joined the party, he has no official positions (unlike Zhang Weiying, he is not the director of a university institute or department). For a decade he held an influential post as editor of *Dushu* – the leading intellectual journal in China – but it was taken away from him with very little notice in advance of the 17th Party Congress in 2007. Although he is a professor at Tsinghua University, Wang Hui has an uncomfortable relationship with the authorities: writing reports exposing local corruption and helping workers organize themselves against illegal privatizations. He often uses the media to put the spotlight on government failings.

Wang Hui is one of the leaders of the 'New Left', a loose grouping of intellectuals that is increasingly capturing the public mood, and setting the tone for political debate. They are 'new' because unlike the 'old left' they support market reforms. They are Left, because unlike the 'New Right' they worry about inequality. Many sought exile in the USA in the 1990s, but now they are back to join the debate about China's future. In an interview, Wang Hui set out their stall: 'China is caught between the two extremes of misguided socialism and crony capitalism, and suffering from the worst elements of both systems ... I am generally in favor of orienting the country toward market reforms, but China's development must be more equal, more balanced. We must not give total priority to GDP growth to the exclusion of worker's rights and the environment.'

Their philosophy is a product of China's relative affluence. Now that the market is driving economic growth, they ask what should be done with the wealth. Should it continue accumulating

33

in the hands of a privileged elite or can China foster a model of development that benefits all its citizens? Thirty years into China's reform process they are challenging the philosophy of growth as the ultimate goal: instead of hurtling towards nineteenth-century laissez-faire capitalism, they want to develop a Chinese variant of social democracy. And while, like magpies, they adapt ideas from all over the world to Chinese conditions, they feel that China's development should be built on Beijing's terms. As Wang Hui says:

> We cannot count on a state on the German or Nordic model. We have such a large country that the state apparatus would have to be vast to provide that kind of welfare. That is why we need institutional innovation. Wang Shaoguang [a political economist] is talking about low-price health-care. Cui Zhiyuan [a political theorist] is talking about socialized capital and reforming property rights to give workers a say over the companies where they work. Hu Angang [an economist] is talking about Green development.

Their goal is to challenge the imported ideas of 'Pearl River Capitalism' and replace them with a home-grown philosophy: 'We have to find an alternate way. This is the great mission of our generation.' And as the list of problems arising from the market grows almost as long as the many achievements, the senior leadership is taking note of their ideas. They are beginning to feel that their time has come.

Yellow River Capitalism

Henan literally means 'South of the River', because of its location on the banks of the Yellow River. This is the heart of inland China, the spiritual opposite of Shenzhen. Traditionally regarded as the birthplace of Chinese civilization, it is also home to a village that became the poster boy of the 'New Left' in the 1990s: Nanjie. In a deliberate experiment, Nanjie's leaders created a synthesis of the market and collectivism, as they abandoned their agricultural heritage to embrace industrialization (the authorities built twenty-six factories making everything from instant noodles to plastic wrappers). Village life in Nanjie is resonant of nineteenth-century experiments in ethical capitalism such as Robert Owen's New Lanark in Britain. The workers are paid above average wages and everyone is given free housing, free healthcare, rations of meat and eggs, and a daily bottle of beer. Primary and even college education is subsidized. The authorities look after the moral welfare of their citizens, not with religious sermons as in New Lanark, but through compulsory study-sessions of Mao's philosophy and regular 'criticism and self-criticism' of each other's behaviour. In 1996, the village was immortalized in a glowing book by the 'New Left' political theorist Cui Zhiyuan.

For him, the village was a living embodiment of an 'alternative way'. It showed that the market could be used to finance social welfare; that success could be achieved in the rural communities of inland provinces rather than only on the coast. And it showed how government intervention – to provide health and education – could improve economic dynamism. Today some of the sheen has come off Nanjie, which is increasingly seen as an artefact rather than a model. But even in 1996, Cui Zhiyuan did not think that Nanjie could be universalized. Instead, he argued that it showed how China could survive in market conditions without slashing the wages, terms and social protection of its workers. It was an emblem of an alternative form of capitalism to that practised in the Pearl River Delta, one which I will call 'Yellow River Capitalism'.

Where Wang Hui speaks slowly and deliberately, Cui Zhiyuan can be exhausting to follow. When he talks his sparkling eyes almost pop out of his head. His delivery is breathless with the enthusiasm of a mad scientist intoxicated by the pursuit of knowledge. As he draws on learned quotations to back up his points, one gets the sense that he is holding the ring for a perpetual argument that is going on in his head between his intellectual mentors: Niccolò Machiavelli, Jean-Jacques Rousseau, John Stuart Mill and James Meade. Cui Zhiyuan is one of the most optimistic members of the 'New Left', seeing experimentation as a key to solving China's problems: 'The present experience of Russia – and the experiences of developing countries around the world – demonstrate that these countries cannot achieve the wealth, strength and freedom of rich industrial democracies by simply imitating the economic and political institutions of these democracies. They must, to succeed, invent different institutions.' For the 'New Left', the key to the Yellow River Capitalism is a philosophy of perpetual innovation – developing new kinds of companies and social institutions that marry competition and co-operation.

The weakest state in the world

'Big state bad, small state good' was the mantra of the economists in the 1980s and 1990s. But the 'New Left' team of Wang Shaoguang and Hu Angang has done much to turn that debate on its head. This odd couple – who had a chance encounter at Yale University – emerged as a sort of Lennon and McCartney for 'New Left' economics in China. In an influential report in the early 1990s, they argued that the Chinese state had the wrong kind of power: despotic rather than governing. Its ability to restrict the personal freedom of its citizens was second to none. However, when it came to running the country in an effective way, China's state was one of the weakest in the world.

They showed that central government's revenue had steadily fallen as a percentage of GDP from 31.2 per cent in 1978 to 14.7 per cent in 1992. As the central state's budget fell, the income of local governments grew and grew, creating a series of 'red barons' in the provinces who used dubious ad hoc charges to line their personal and provincial coffers and increase their power. By the end of the 1980s, the 'red barons' had become as powerful as the central government.

For the 'New Left', almost all of the problems hampering China's reforms – corruption, overheating of the economy, bad investment, non-performing loans, low levels of domestic consumption and growing inequality – had come about because the central government was too weak, rather than too strong.

Hu Angang estimates that the combined costs of illegal bribes, tax evasion, arbitrary local charges and straightforward theft add up to a staggering 15 per cent of China's GDP every year. He shows how, without democratic accountability from below or fear of sanctions from above, provincial leaders put their own interests above those of the people, spending most of their extra-budgetary revenue on themselves and their families: higher salaries, cars, air-conditioning, refrigerators and shiny new office buildings. The solution, according to him, was to centralize the collection of taxes in order to prevent the proliferation of arbitrary charges and to create central institutions to tackle corruption.

The 'New Left' made a similar argument about the expensive white elephants such as luxury hotels, skyscrapers, state-of-the-art amusement parks and giant stadiums which local governments have become addicted to building. These unproductive investments, which contribute to an overheating of the economy, are built with money from China's banks which Deng Xiaoping had freed from central control.

However, their most powerful argument is that a stronger state could help stimulate higher household consumption which currently stands less than 40 per cent of GDP, the lowest of any major economy. The 'New Left' claim that China's model of development is unsustainable because there is a limit to the amount of goods and services that the rest of the world will be able to buy, so China will need to start consuming more of its own products. In the future, China will quite simply need to spend more, and save less. The 'New Left' correctly argue that domestic consumption will only rise when Chinese citizens feel less insecure. As long as there is no welfare state to protect Chinese citizens from illness, unemployment or old age they will save their money for the future, rather than spending it as they earn it. The 'New Left' claim that only a revitalized central government can provide the social safety net which would give Chinese citizens the confidence to consume. Their words have not fallen on deaf ears. The percentage of central government tax revenue has been gradually increased since 1994, and – rhetorically at least – Hu Jintao and Wen Jiabao have committed themselves to rebuild China's welfare state.

Protecting public property

'Property is theft' has been one of the Left's favourite expressions ever since Pierre-Joseph Proudhon first coined the phrase in 1840. But while the French anarchist was speaking primarily in conceptual terms, in China it is literally true. The 'New Left' talk of a new 'enclosure movement' – referring to the way that private landlords grabbed common land in England between the twelfth and nineteenth centuries – that is ripping up China's social protection system and creating mass inequality. Every week newspapers and websites carry stories of party bigwigs carving up and plundering the nation's assets under the cover of privatization. Property that was once taken from the rich and given to the peasants is confiscated from farmers and given to developers. Entire villages have been forced off their land to allow property speculators to build new developments; factories have been sold at knock-down rates so that their assets could be stripped and plundered. These cases have seen corrupt officials and crooked businessmen become overnight millionaires while the workers and land-owners whose assets they appropriated received derisory amounts of compensation.

The three letters that have come to symbolize the most brazen pillaging of collective resources are 'MBO', short for management buyout. In 2004, a little-known Hong Kong-based academic called Lang Xianping became a national figure when he used his slot on an obscure local Shanghai TV station to investigate and expose some of these abuses. His show caused such waves that Gu Chujun, the chairman of one of the companies that he exposed, took him to court for defamation with a plucky battle-cry 'I'm fighting for the honour of the entrepreneurs.' Before Gu Chujun lost his case and was put in prison, the economist Zhang Weiying came to his defence, complaining about the practice of 'monsterizing and vilifying entrepreneurs' and arguing that privatization should continue both for reasons of efficiency and principle. He argued that State Owned Enterprises will never take risks because their managers are appointed by bureaucrats; only capitalist entrepreneurs will create new wealth. Even if there are some irregularities in the privatization process, he claimed, it is a price worth paying because China will only be able to develop when the state has retreated from the economy, and its biggest companies are in private hands. Privatization will benefit all.

The 'New Left' disagree that state-owned companies will necessarily underperform, arguing that they too can recruit professional managers from the market who could be rewarded or punished according to their performance. What worries the 'New Left' most are the social costs of privatization. State Owned Enterprises, for better or worse, provided an 'Iron Rice Bowl' for their workers: as well as paying workers a salary, they organized education, pensions, housing, healthcare and even sport. Privatization and economic restructuring has not just deprived millions of workers of jobs, it has stripped them of the social protection that made their families' lives viable as well. The fact that China has gone from full employment to a situation where there are 40–60 million unemployed – as well as tens of millions of migrant workers (*mingnong*) who live as exiles in their own country with no rights because they have no certificate of residence – has led to work becoming a commodity. The Chinese political elite have been divided for over a decade over the idea of introducing a law to protect private property. Wang Hui talks for many in the 'New Left' when he says 'we have nothing against protecting private property, but shouldn't we also have a law to protect public property?'

Cui Zhiyuan has an even more radical idea: a new way of sharing the profits of China's State Owned Enterprises. China's 169 biggest companies declared net profits of over 600 billion Yuan ($75 billion) in 2005. But in spite of their enormous profits China's state companies do not pay dividends to their main shareholder: the state. The government is finally preparing to ask these firms to pay up. However, Cui Zhiyuan wants them to give the dividends to the people rather than the government. His model comes not from China's socialist past, but from Alaska. Since 1982, the government of this bleak polar state has used some of the income generated by its massive oil reserves to set up a giant trust fund for its citizens, paying them a 'social dividend' worth thousands of dollars every year. Cui Zhiyuan argues that profits of State Owned Enterprises should be treated like Alaskan oil, going to the mass of Chinese people rather than a wealthy elite. He claims that this social wage would help to remove Chinese insecurity, allow citizens to take low-paying jobs and increase domestic consumption.

Green Cat Development

China's 'New Left' do not just worry about the social impact of China's breakneck development; they also worry about an environmental nightmare. On my own visits to Beijing, I always know when my plane has entered Chinese airspace: the pollution is so bad that I cannot see the ground. China's air, water and land are being laid waste by the country's relentless pursuit of economic growth. As development advances from the eastern coasts, the hinterland is becoming a barren, hellish wasteland – the poorest regions have been transformed into a dumping ground for industrial detritus. Two-thirds of China's electricity comes from dirty coal, with a new coal-fired plant built every week. China's factories blurt out toxic fumes and dump chemicals and waste in the rivers and lakes. Chinese agriculture uses fertilizers that are banned in the rest of the world. Already a quarter of China's land has turned to desert, as a result of deforestation, and this is spreading at a rate of 2,460 km a year. As a result 30 per cent of China has acid rain; 75 per cent of lakes are polluted and rivers are contaminated or pumped dry; and nearly 700 million people drink water contaminated with animal and human waste. There is a shortage of arable land, as millions of peasants find that their fields are confiscated for development or contaminated by chemicals.

The growth-at-all-costs incentive structure for local officials was enshrined when Deng Xiaoping said, 'It doesn't matter if the cat is black or white. All that matters is that it catches mice.' Economic growth, therefore, should come before any kind of ideology. The 'New Left', on the other hand, argue that the colour of the cat does matter. Hu Angang says that the growth for the last twenty years has been 'Black Cat GDP growth'. He has been advocating ways of measuring growth that take out the costs of environmental destruction. He calls this 'Green Cat Development'. Attacking the 1980s model of 'getting rich first, clearing up later', Hu Angang argues that China's economic restructuring should allow it to avoid the Western model of building growth on high resource consumption and high pollution by using taxes, tax-breaks and regulation to encourage greater efficiency, renewable energy and a new generation of 'Green Jobs'.

These ideas gained momentum with the promotion of the dynamic and mercurial young princeling Pan Yue to head SEPA, the State Environmental Protection Administration. Pan Yue, the son-in-law of Liu Huaqing, a former PLA general who served on the Politburo, brought Hu Angang's dream closer to reality by publishing the first official report on China's 'Green GDP' in 2006. His report showed that air, water and solid-waste pollution caused US$64 billion worth of damage across China in 2004, accounting for 3.05 per cent of the year's gross domestic product. The 'Green GDP' calculation system is based on the cost of using five natural resources – land, minerals, forest, water and fisheries – and the cost of environmental pollution and ecological damage. Pan Yue explained that this measure was only 'the tip of the iceberg'. Pan Yue's activities have been dismissed as tokenism – his tiny agency is not a match for the massive incentive structure that compels authorities at all levels of government to put growth above a concern for the environment. But he has tried to make up for a lack of political clout with an appeal to a still nascent civic society, calling for public hearings on big development projects so that citizens can discuss their fears of the environmental consequences of major building projects. And, while most officials of vice-ministerial rank tend to keep a low profile and avoid the Western media and non-governmental organizations like the plague, Pan Yue is rarely out of the limelight. Wearing his trademark black suit and shirt – no tie – he has often used the domestic and foreign media, as well as NGOs such as Greenpeace and the World Wildlife Fund, to take on power companies and local polluters. Pan Yue has talked of 'China's environmental suicide' and in an interview with the German magazine, *Der Spiegel*, predicted that 'China's economic miracle will end soon because the environment can no longer keep pace'.

Pan Yue's colourful statement hints at the fact that for China's leaders it is the indirect effects of pollution which are most disturbing. They worry about the economic burden it imposes on growth, the costs of deteriorating public health, and the threat to the country's international reputation of being seen as a climate villain. Most alarming for them is the threat of social instability. According to China's top environmental official, Zhou Shengxian, there were 51,000 pollution-related protests in 2005 – some of which attracted tens of thousands of people. Beijing is now talking tough on pollution, and has set ambitious targets to protect the environment. But as Wang Shaoguang and Hu Angang have argued, the power of the central state is limited. In spite of some promising local experiments such as the building of a 'zero-carbon city' in Dongtan near Shanghai, the overall picture remains bleak. When it comes to implementation, local officials pay less attention to environmental targets than to the imperative of growth. And, because of the complaints of local leaders, Pan Yue's Green GDP reporting has been quietly shelved. The environmentalists of the 'New Left' may have won the battle of ideas in Beijing, but it is more traditional goals such as the quest for profits that are winning out on the ground.

The turn to the Left

You would imagine that Zhang Weiying would be on a high. He has been part of the most successful economic experiment of the last century. He is handsomely paid for his company directorships. He has a senior post in one of the most prestigious academic institutions in China. But for all his fame, money, and professional success, when I last visited Zhang Weiying – in the summer of 2006 – he was not a happy man.

The last two decades have seen a process of *Gaizhi*, a Chinese term meaning 'transforming the system', where many enterprises have been restructured, and often privatized. A decade ago there were 300,000 State Owned Enterprises compared to just 150,000 today. At the same time employment in these firms has been cut by 40 per cent, or 45 million jobs. But for Zhang Weiying, this process has not gone far enough. His main gripe is that decisions about who runs State Owned Enterprises are still taken by the Communist Party's personnel departments. These party officials do not have the incentives to appoint entrepreneurs. 'Bureaucrats, unlike their capitalist counterparts,' Zhang Weiying explains, 'do not bear risks for their selections.'

Zhang Weiying is facing up to the fundamental problem of his invention: the fact that dual-track transition keeps the old system in place for a long time. Three decades into the reform era, China's industrial base is still dominated by the state sector (the state owns 60 per cent of China's fixed capital stock and 80 per cent of the chief executives of state enterprises are appointed by the party).

Although China has a vibrant stock market – the combined size of Shanghai and Shenzhen exchanges would make them eighth in the world – barely a third of the market's shares are permitted to trade. The highest-profile corporations – like China Mobile or Sinopec – are controlled by the state. Even private companies that trade on global markets – such as Lenovo – are connected to the government through shady networks.

From Zhang Weiying's perspective, the country is full of half-completed reforms – painted horses rather than zebras. He thinks that after three decades of extraordinary growth, the time has come to admit that China is a village of zebras – and to banish the remaining horses.

Zhang Weiying fears that the government has lost its drive to see the process through to its logical conclusion, to write itself out of the economic picture. Economic growth is now taken for granted, rather than seen as the most urgent goal. Fewer of the State Owned Enterprises are losing money, so the pressure to privatize has eased. And political leaders in Beijing now talk about the need to stop the economy overheating, to redistribute wealth, to achieve 'balanced development', rather than the need to accelerate growth of privatization. Zhang Weiying and his 'New Right' colleagues worry that President Hu Jintao and Prime Minister Wen Jiabao have succumbed to a dangerous form of populism. They worry that measures to redistribute wealth will slow economic growth – and in the process threaten the achievements of the last thirty years. In an economy where many have made their fortunes through dubious means, they worry that the drive against corruption could lead the government to follow Vladimir Putin's Russian model of confiscating assets from business oligarchs.

Zhang Weiying longs for the days of Deng Xiaoping, Jiang Zemin and Zhu Rongji who suppressed discussions about inequality, glorying in the fact that 'some will get rich first': 'During a reform process you need leaders who are missionary. Today is very different from the 1980s and 1990s. At central and local level the leaders are not missionary. They worry too much about public opinion.' Public opinion is turning Zhang Weiying's world upside down. The debate of the 1980s between conservatives and reformers has been won by reformers. The decision to open up and reform seems irreversible. However, a new debate has opened up in its place: what kind of reforms should China pursue? Who will benefit from them? How can the profits of growth be shared? Websites, newspapers and TV stations no longer debate how to dismantle the state. Their big question is about how to tame the market. Zhang Weiying can feel his power drifting away. He complains that he and his colleagues are 'under siege', attacked by the Left on websites and denounced in the media: 'It is very hard to discuss serious issues in this climate. In the 1980s and 1990s we could talk amongst economists. But today ordinary people use left-wing rhetoric to attack us. They destroy our credibility by saying we are sponsored by the US government or the new capitalist class. We feel like scholars taking on soldiers.'

The New Machiavelli and the Harmonious Society

In today's China, the battle of ideas has become entwined with the pursuit of raw power. Behind its monolithic façade, the Communist hierarchy has been caught up in an increasingly rancorous struggle for the soul of the party, with two political gangs associating themselves with the ideas of the 'New Left' and the 'New Right'.

The 'New Leftist' Cui Zhiyuan draws on a surprising source to explain these shifting political dynamics: mediaeval Europe. Many Western observers, he says, struggle to make sense of China because they see politics as the relationship between governors and the governed, between the state and civil society. But Cui Zhiyuan claims that the struggles which so baffle modern Europeans would have been immediately recognizable to inhabitants of mediaeval Europe like Niccolò Machiavelli:

> For Machiavelli power was not divided between two levels: the state and the people. Florentine politics was split between three groups: the prince (the 'one'), the nobles (the 'few') and the people (the 'many'). In today's China, the 'one' is the Communist Party, the 'few' are the super-rich, and the 'many' are the people. Machiavelli shows how the 'one' and the 'few' can collude against the 'many', but also how the ruler can make common cause with the people against nobility.

According to Cui Zhiyuan, Chinese politics in the 1980s was a protracted love affair between the party and the super-rich, as Mao Zedong's plea to 'serve the people' gave way to Deng Xiaoping's alleged injunction that 'to get rich is glorious'. Deng Xiaoping's chosen successor, the former Shanghai party boss Jiang Zemin, went even further with his so-called 'three represents' theory that invited private entrepreneurs to join the Communist Party on the grounds that it should represent economic production as well as social and cultural forces. Jiang Zemin assembled around him a clique from the affluent coastal regions that continued to hold power after he retired. Because Jiang Zemin's powerbase is in Shanghai, they are often known as the 'Shanghai set', which also reflects their fascination with the most avant-garde experiments in Chinese capitalism. Like their 'New Right' friends in academia, such as Zhang Weiying, the Shanghai set supports fast economic growth, a relatively high degree of provincial autonomy in economic affairs, loose controls on investment and bank lending and close ties between the party and the country's rising class of private businessmen.

However, since 2002 the 'New Right' consensus has been challenged by President Hu Jintao. He has built an alternative powerbase around the Chinese Communist Youth League (CCYL); the so-called *tuanpai* who cut their teeth in the less developed inland provinces. They sing more from the 'New Left' hymn sheet, advocating slower and more stable growth, greater attention to social inequality and pollution, and an expansion of state support for education, medical care and social security. Hu Jintao's catch-phrases of 'Harmonious Society' and 'Scientific Development' stand for a range of policies intended to restore a balance between the country's thriving market economy and its neglected socialistpast.

Instead of cosying up to big business, President Hu Jintao together with Prime Minister Wen Jiabao, has made overtures to the workers, peasants and the dispossessed; trying to ally himself with the 'many' against the 'few'. Through a series of media stunts – such as sleeping in the houses of peasants and interceding on behalf of workers who were not getting paid – he has differentiated himself from the 'elitist policies' of Jiang Zemin. Most worrying for the 'New Right' is the shift away from growth as the overriding objective for China. At a heated meeting of the Politburo in July 2004, the former party boss of Shanghai Chen Liangyu allegedly pointed his finger at Wen Jiabao and warned him that he would be held responsible if policies designed to slow growth in the eastern coastal provinces – in order to redistribute money to the western inland provinces – led to political turmoil. Chen

Liangyu, an enthusiastic free-marketeer, set out the 'New Right' credo when he said that 'when the Sun rises, it shines first on the East. It doesn't shine on the East and West at the same time ... Balanced development does not mean robbing the rich to help the poor; robbing the rich to help the poor would leave all equally poor, not equally rich ... Our party-state's historic experience with economic building proved long ago that egalitarian thinking will only strangle development.'

China's political system is not one where the winner takes all. Each of the two factions needs the other to define itself, and power is finely balanced between them. Hu Jintao seemed to be in the ascendant when he engineered the high-profile sacking – on corruption charges – of Chen Liangyu in 2006. But when it came to elections to the Politburo's Standing Committee at the five-yearly Party Congress in October 2007, the two factions got roughly the same number of slots, and Hu Jintao failed to get his protégé Li Keqiang anointed as his successor.

In policy terms, however, the balance of power is subtly shifting towards the Left. At the end of 2005, Hu Jintao and Wen Jiabao published the '11th Five Year Plan', their blueprint for a 'Harmonious Society'. This report – based on the research of dozens of teams of party officials sent to examine social policy in Europe, the USA, Latin America, East Asia and Africa – marked a clear shift in the way the country thinks about its economic future. For the first time since the reform era began in 1978, economic growth was not described as the overriding goal for the Chinese state. In its place was a broader goal of 'development' which China's leaders now define as 'putting people first' (*yiren weiben*) while respecting the natural environment. They talked about introducing a Scandinavian model of social welfare with promises of a 20 per cent year-on-year increase in the funds available for pensions, unemployment benefit, health insurance and maternity leave. For rural China they promised a 'New Socialist Countryside' where arbitrary taxes would be cut, and health and education improved. They also pledged to reduce energy consumption per unit of GDP by 20 per cent, and to introduce new performance indicators for party officials that stress social and environmental indicators as well as economic growth. China's shift in policy orientation was further sealed when the 2007 Party Congress enshrined Hu Jintao's Left-leaning 'Scientific Development Concept' in the party's constitution at the same level as Mao Zedong Thought and Deng Xiaoping Thought, an achievement that eluded his predecessor Jiang Zemin while he was in office.

Although the details are still being worked through, the 11th Five Year Plan is a template for Yellow River Capitalism. From Zhang Weiying and the early reformers, it preserves the idea of permanent experimentation – a gradualist reform process rather than shock therapy. It accepts their belief that the market rather than the state will drive economic growth. From the 'New Left', it draws a concern about inequality and the environment, and a quest for new institutions that can marry co-operation with competition. By stressing the state's obligation to divide the proceeds of growth and deliver social services, it mounts a direct challenge to the 'flat world' philosophy of laissez-faire capitalist development. This promise of delivering rapid economic growth whilst maintaining state control is turning Yellow River Capitalism into a beacon for developing governments around the world. China may not have set out to overturn the dominance of Anglo-Saxon economics, but if the next phase of the Chinese economic miracle takes off it could once again turn the world's thinking about economic development on its head.

CHAPTER TWO

Democracy in the Clouds

Western democracy is like going to a restaurant and choosing whether you want a French, Italian or German chef who will decide on your behalf what is on the menu. With Chinese democracy we always have the same chef – the Communist Party – but we will increasingly get to choose which dishes he cooks.

Fang Ning, Chinese Academy of Social Sciences

Pingchang is a city in the clouds. Over five hours' drive down meandering mountainous roads from the Sichuanese capital Chengdu, it floats at 600 metres above sea-level in the Daba mountain range. The countryside around it is stunning – a luxuriant palette of greens embodied in trees, grasses, bamboo and crops. Terraces have been carved out of the mountainside to grow rice and grain. The roads weave in and out of the mist, revealing the contours of a town perched on the edge of a deep ravine. The brutalism of its concrete housing blocks hits arriving travellers like a slap in the face. Its shabby silhouette juts out from the rock of the mountain like a socialist realist pastiche of the Disney Castle. Prince Charles would have called it a carbuncle, but I was moved by the utopianism of its already anachronistic vision of modernity. Even in its dilapidated condition it signalled man's ambition to impose his will on nature.

Most of Pingchang's residents live in villages connected to the town centre by muddy tracks. In Nun Chao, the first village I came to, peasants laden with makeshift yokes and wicker backpacks walked under large red street banners proclaiming the creation of 'a new socialist countryside'. But Nun Chao did not seem to be very new. Its decaying houses – inhabited only by the old, the frail and the sick – reminded me of TV footage of war zones. Without any introduction, an elderly lady came up to tell me that the village had been a shell since the able-bodied men emigrated to work as labourers (those left behind to tend the fields, she said, make just RMB 900 (£65) a year).

While we were talking, a crowd of world-weary, ruddy-faced peasants gathered around us speaking in excited tones of their problems: falling incomes from fields, rising fees for doctors and schools, the lack of male role models for the children, the loneliness of their dislocated lives. Within minutes there were dozens of villagers shouting louder and louder in a chorus of impotent rage. They all entreated me to carry their messages of anguish back to Beijing. Little did they know that my friends in Beijing had sent me to study Pingchang as a model for the future of China.

Incremental democracy

Pingchang County is attracting a lot of visitors these days – but they are not coming to see the beauty of its architecture, or the success of its economic model. They come because Pingchang is the first county in China where party members have been allowed to elect the party secretaries of their townships in competitive ballots. The experiment is pretty novel in a party where advancement depends more on loyalty and personal connections than the preferences of ordinary members. In normal circumstances, each layer of government simply appoints the leaders on the next rung down – the national party picks the leaders of the provincial parties who, in turn, recruit the leaders of the prefectures, who choose county leaders, who can appoint township leaders, who themselves are responsible for selecting the leaders of the village parties. Pingchang threatens to turn this process on its head. It is the most advanced experiment of what Chinese thinkers call 'inner-party democracy'. When I went to investigate it in 2006, the county's party secretary, Liu Qian Xiang, proudly explained that the elections have put Pingchang on the map: 'Our economy is not well developed but our experiments in democracy are.'

I first heard about Pingchang from a friend who works for the Central Compilation and Translation Bureau. The unpromising name belongs to an august institution which was established in the 1930s to introduce socialist thinking to the Chinese: translating classical texts such as *Das Kapital*, the *Communist Manifesto* and Lenin's *What is to be Done* into Chinese. It was one of the key organs of the Communist Party even before the People's Republic itself was established. After the reform era started in 1978, the Bureau struggled to find a new role. Unlike the well-funded think-tanks with sparkling new buildings, the Bureau is located next to a grocery store with fruit and vegetables that pour out on to the street and a Chinese greasy spoon that has become a Mecca for local workers breakfasting on red-bean dumplings and eggs. But now the Bureau has found a new sense of purpose. Its shabby buildings house a powerhouse of ideas, the 'Local Government Innovation and Excellence Award'.

The Bureau's deputy director, Yu Keping, is a rising star who is spoken of as an informal adviser to President Hu Jintao. After completing a PhD at Beijing University, he became head of a new institute within the Bureau – part university, part think-tank, part 'McKinsey' for government reform. He has an easy manner, an open and informal style and a good command of English, picked up on his many visits to the West, including a spell as a visiting fellow at Duke University in the USA. Yu Keping is like the Zhang Weiying of political reform – painting political horses all over the country in the hope that experiments in grass-roots democracy could one day eclipse China's dictatorship. He hopes that grass-roots experiments like Pingchang will become the Shenzhens of democratic politics.

His centre's flagship project is an award programme for innovations in local democracy: 'Many think-tanks and groups of experts are brainstorming on reform inside the Communist Party and within government institutions. Local and spontaneous initiatives are numerous. We try to survey, assess and compare them. The best ideas are rewarded with prizes.' Since the programme started in 1999, some 800 projects have been nominated and thirty prizes have been handed out to reward market-oriented reforms, elections of township leaders and democratic consultations. The winners attract national attention. For example, when the Pingchang County elections won a prize in 2006, the county found itself overrun by eighty-six groups of researchers who came to study the experiment. China's deputy president even asked for a personal briefing on the county's elections.

Yu Keping caused waves in December 2006 when he wrote an article in the Central Party School's newspaper called 'Democracy is a Good Thing' which claimed that 'even if people have the best food, clothing, housing and transport but no democratic rights they still do not have complete human dignity'. But Yu Keping has avoided getting swept up in crackdowns on political dissent by focusing on specific, small-scale projects, rather than indulging in grand rhetoric about freedom and human rights. His big idea is the modest-sounding 'incremental democracy', which rejects a big bang of political reform in favour of gradualist change from the bottom up. Drawing a direct analogy with the economic realm, he says that overnight reform would be as damaging to China as economic 'shock therapy'. For many years, Yu Keping has instead promoted the idea of a democratic cascade that would see democracy gradually work its way up from successful grass-roots experiments. Elections should be held first in the 700,000 villages, and then at the higher levels of government – the 38,000 townships, 2,500 counties, 330 prefectures and the thirty-four provinces – before impinging on the politics of central government.

Yu Keping's cascade got off to a promising start when the Chinese commune system was dissolved in the 1980s, and elections were introduced for village committees. By 1994, half of Chinese villages had held elections. In 1998, elections were made compulsory for all villages through the Organic Law for Village Committees (OLVC). In the same year, a small township in Sichuan called Buyun made history by becoming the first township – the next level of government up from a village – to hold a direct competitive election for its leaders that was open to all residents. In 2001, the election for the head of the township was repeated (although this time the candidate chosen by citizens had to be ratified by the township 'People's Congress'). Yu Keping argues that the election had a profound impact on local life. When he presented Buyun with a prize in 2004, he claimed that 'village voters have recognized their democratic rights . . . the township leader has a much improved sense of responsibility and accountability . . . Promises made when running for election have largely been realized by the time of the term election.' Every month in Buyun, he explained, there is a 'Township leader reception day' where people can raise concerns on local issues, and once a year, on the eve of the lunar new year, the township leader gives a progress report to all the citizens of the town.

But since the heady days of the late 1990s, the onward march of democracy has stalled, with only a handful of other townships following Buyun's lead. And what is more, even at a village level many elections have a single candidate rather than a genuine competition. Among Chinese intellectuals there is widespread cynicism about the importance of village elections. They claim that village committees have very few resources, no public money and are only responsible for trivial matters. Yu Keping and his colleagues retort that this is metropolitan snobbishness: although local elected officials in Beijing have little impact on citizens' lives, in the countryside they are responsible for crucial policy objectives such as family planning, taxation and land acquisition. Yu Keping's claims are backed up in research by the economist Yang Yao of Beijing University, which shows that elections can help to tackle corruption and improve public services. In a study that looked at forty-eight villages over sixteen years, Yao Yang found that the introduction of elections had increased spending on public services by 20 per cent, while reducing the proportion spent on 'administrative costs' (bureaucratic speak for the entertainment budgets and salaries of local bosses and their families) by 18 per cent.

The biggest problem for these elections is the role of the Communist Party. In China, every government post is shadowed by a party position which ensures that the office-holders stick to the party line. According to the critics, this parallel structure makes direct elections meaningless because village committees are forced to serve two masters: the people that elect them, and the party. When the two conflict, the interests of the party usually win out. Yu Keping accepts that this is a more valid criticism. That is why he has recently become so excited by the Pingchang election – an attempt to introduce democracy into the heart of the Communist Party. Because the party controls everything, he argues, there is hope that if it can be made democratic it will change the nature of the country. Yu Keping's assessment may be a little over-optimistic, but his idea of 'inner party democracy' is catching on.

Inner party democracy

Pingchang County is Yu Keping's equivalent of the village of zebras. It shows how closely his ideas for the political realm resemble Zhang Weiying's theories on economic reform. Yu Keping hopes that by promoting democracy first within the party, it will then spread to the rest of society. Just as the coastal regions were allowed to 'get rich first', Yu Keping thinks that party members should 'get democracy first' by having elections within the Communist Party. Where the coastal regions benefited from natural economic advantages such as proximity to Hong Kong, Cantonese language and transport links, Yu Keping sees advantages for party members – such as their high levels of education and articulacy – which make them into a natural democratic vanguard. In his eyes, the Pingchang experiment could point the way for an incremental reform of party structures.

So what would inner party democracy mean in practice? In broad terms it would mean strengthening the rights of ordinary party members to stand for election, vote for their representatives and scrutinize elected officials. The idea would be to rejuvenate the party from the bottom up by insisting on competitive elections for all party posts. In recent years this has begun with the votes for provincial and national party congresses where the electoral slates have had 15–30 per cent more candidates than positions, but these congresses are more rubber-stamping bodies than serious centres of power. In the long run, 'inner party democracy' could be extended to the upper echelons of the party, including competitive elections for the most senior posts such as party chief. The logical conclusion of these ideas on inner party democracy would be for the Communist Party itself to eventually split into different factions that competed on ideological slates for support. It is not impossible to imagine informal 'New Left' and 'New Right' groupings one day even becoming formal parties within the party.

There was a lively debate about inner party democracy in advance of the 2007 Party Congress because the Vietnamese Communist Party – whose structure has historically been modelled on China's – decided to introduce competitive elections for their own party chief earlier that year. Although the Chinese Communist Party decided not to follow suit this time, the 17th Party Congress did move in the direction of greater participation. According to newspaper reports, the anointment of the Shanghai party boss Xi Jinping as the front-runner to become Hu Jintao's successor was influenced by a secret poll of Communist Party officials. Although Hu Jintao had been grooming the Liaoning party boss Li Keqiang to take over, his favoured candidate was apparently roundly defeated in the poll by Xi Jinping.

Yu Keping's ideas could have a profound impact on China: if the Communist Party were a country, its 70 million members would make it bigger than the UK. And yet, his political project seems a long way from reality. It is hard to imagine the remote, impoverished county of Pingchang becoming a model for the gleaming metropolises of Shanghai, Beijing or Shenzhen. And, so far, none of the other 2,499 counties of China have followed its lead. What is more, the very fact that political reformers such as Yu Keping have to trawl the most obscure parts of rural China for experiments in grass-roots democracy shows how inhospitable the climate for discussing political reform within China has become. From the public discussions of China's intellectuals you would never guess that less than two hours' flight from Shanghai there is a Chinese society – one which the Chinese state even claims is an integral part of China – that has multi-party elections, freedom of speech, a growing human rights culture and a per capita GDP of $30,000 a year. However, because of official propaganda and the sensitivity about Taiwanese independence, it is more acceptable for scholars such as Yu Keping to draw on indigenous experiments within China than lessons from Taiwan.

Yu Keping's technocratic approach is a sign of the times. In the 1970s students built a 'democracy wall' in Beijing by creating big character posters that called for free elections. In the 1980s, they would argue over which political system China should embrace when it eventually became a democracy. Would it adopt an American Presidential system with a strict division of powers between a legislature, an executive and a judiciary? Or would a Westminster model of democracy – with the government being elected by the parliament – be more appropriate to the Chinese situation? Others wanted to plump for a hybrid system – maybe based on the French model. This debate reached its apotheosis with the student demonstrations in Tiananmen Square in 1989. There are many reforms being canvassed, but since Tiananmen the hope of China moving towards multi-party elections has all but disappeared. The propaganda department stops the media from using words like 'human rights' and 'freedom'; and debates about separating the party from the government have been more or less banned.

Yu Keping explains that the debate on political reform of the 1980s – which focused on multi-party elections, liberalization and the separation of power – is giving way to a new one which is much more modest. In the past, intellectuals were divided about the sequencing of reform – should economic follow political reform, or should it be the other way around? But today they argue about what the ultimate destination should be. Reform is seen less through the prism of human rights and freedom, than the question of how to increase the legitimacy of the ruling Communist Party. Instead of trying to develop a Chinese variant of liberal democracy, many intellectuals are looking for a different model altogether.

Democracy = chaos

'You talk about democracy as if it were a religion which needs to be spread around the world. But elections will not solve any of the problems facing China today.' This is how Pan Wei, a rising star at Beijing University, greeted me at our first meeting, castigating me for paying so much attention to the experiments in grass-roots democracy that have sprung up around China. 'The Sichuan experiment will go nowhere,' he says, 'the local leaders have their personal political goal: they want to make their names known. But the experiment has not succeeded. In fact, Sichuan is the place with the highest number of mass protests. Very few other places want to emulate them.'

Unfortunately Pan Wei is probably right. In the 1980s and 1990s many scholars argued that democracy was the necessary prerequisite for wider political and economic progress. In particular, it was seen by many as a precondition for growth. But in recent years – not least because of China's own economic success – this link has been increasingly questioned. It is this instrumental view of democracy – as a route to prosperity or political stability rather than a goal in itself – which allows Pan Wei to attack it head on. He argues that elections will not fix any of China's most pressing problems: the rise in protests, the gap between rich and poor, the near bankruptcy of the rural economy, the lack of domestic consumption, or the pervasive corruption of the political elite. In fact, Pan Wei thinks that democracy would actually make things worse: 'The more electorates politicians want to reach, the more money they need. There are always rich people who want to provide money in exchange for some government support. Therefore, once elected, the public officers are to serve electors on the one hand and money providers on the other.' The pressing issue for most people, he says, is not 'who should run the government?', but 'how should the government be run?' He argues that political reform should flow from social problems rather than universal or Western principles.

Most theorists of democracy would not accept Pan Wei's attempt to separate how a government is run from how its leaders are selected: the former is very much a product of the latter. And the legitimacy that comes from elections would strengthen any government that tried to deal with China's problems – domestically and internationally. However, Pan Wei's aversion to democracy seems to have deeper roots than intellectual arguments. He claims that democracy conjures up three of the most painful images in the Chinese psyche: the collapse of the former Soviet Union which followed Gorbachev's political liberalization; the so-called 'people's democracy' of China's own Cultural Revolution; and the risk of an independent Taiwan.

The Soviet Union provided a blueprint for Mao as he set about creating a socialist state in China. The institutions of government, the slogans and the iconography were imported wholesale and given only the slightest Chinese characteristics. During the Cold War, Russia always had a technological edge over China and seemed destined to continue to be the People's Republic's bigger brother for eternity. In 1991, it was exposed as a paper tiger. When

Gorbachev was ejected from power the Soviet empire dissolved into its constituent parts, mafia capitalism shared out the spoils of the economy and the country's GDP was halved. The Chinese ruling elite are in no doubt about why this happened: the mistake of embracing political reform before the economy had been liberalized. They have vowed not to make the same mistake.

Even more painful is the memory of the Cultural Revolution. Launched by Mao in 1966, this attempt to purge China of its bourgeois elements plunged the country into a decade of violent chaos, crippling its economy, destroying its social infrastructure and killing at least half a million people. Many of today's intellectuals spent those years in the countryside – down mines, in factories, or on farms – robbed of their childhood and their educations. Recently I had dinner with a leading Chinese public intellectual who is liberal by inclination and educated in the West, but – because of his experiences of the Cultural Revolution – terrified of the consequences of democracy. His account of his experiences is all too typical for his generation:

I was very idealistic when I was young . . . I wanted to be a noble revolutionary. I went to the countryside and spent ten years doing hard labour in a factory. I did really dirty jobs, risking my life. Sometimes I had ten blisters on my hands. I thought the peasants were masters of history, that they were noble and that we should reform ourselves to be like them (I came from a family of intellectuals). But I found that they are just human like the rest of us. I saw groups of pupils torturing their teachers to death to punish them for giving them bad marks. I had to organize classmates to protect our own teachers from attacks. If you loosen up and open the box, the people will become an uncontrollable mob. So the only hope is top-down reform. This is very difficult but it is possible. In England during the Glorious Revolution and Victorian times there were powerful vested interests, but they realized that reform was in their long-term interests.

Pan Wei, too, fears that elections would let the genie out of the bottle again – pitting impoverished peasants against the country's growing middle class, and causing the country to dissolve into its constituent parts: 'In China, class struggle in the 1960s and 70s turned out to be a Hobbesian war of all against all. None of the involved parties respected or accepted any legal procedure, and the losers would not gracefully accept their failure but fought to the bloody end.'

It is, however, Taiwan which brings out Pan Wei's most colourful language. This island, which China views as a breakaway province, was run under autocratic rule by the anti-Communist Kuomintang for almost fifty years before holding its first free Presidential elections in 1996, thereby showing that Chinese culture and democracy are compatible. But against the evidence, Pan Wei repeatedly represents the country as an economic and political basket-case, brought to its knees by these very elections. He talks about recent corruption scandals involving President Chen Shui-Bian and his family, about how China is rapidly catching up with its neighbour in economic terms, and about the heavily personalized, tabloid politics of this young democracy. He claims that it is democracy that has driven the creation of a Taiwanese national identity. What makes the Chinese so neuralgic about Taiwan's political system is the correct assessment that the Taiwanese would vote for independence were they not living under the Damoclean sword of a Chinese military threat. And what is true of Taiwan could turn out to be true of each of the other Chinese minorities. Would Tibetans vote for independence? What about the Uighurs of Xinjian? China, like the former Soviet

Union, is more of an empire than a nation state. And the experience of the USSR is seen as proof that democracy could lead to the break-up of the nation. For Pan Wei, like many in the Chinese elite, democracy means chaos: 'In the West there is a tradition of power politics. But I don't support a political system that encourages different interests to fight a political struggle where each group tries to grab power. In China the losers would never accept this system.'

It is hard to make out how much of his discourse stems from his instinct for self-preservation and how much is a product of absorbing the government's relentless propaganda. Either way, I find it hard to recognize the vibrant young democracy with a per capita GDP ten times the size of China's from his remarks. Taiwan has many problems, but its political turbulence is not dissimilar to that experienced by other young democracies such as the countries of Central and Eastern Europe. Even the colourful corruption scandals that have enveloped the president and his entourage are a sign of improvement – under the old autocratic systems they would have been kept firmly under wraps. The spread of the rule of law may be lagging behind democracy in Taiwan, but the infrastructure of democracy and the transparency of a free media are powerful antidotes to corruption.

Meritocracy vs. majority rule

Pan Wei berates Westerners for misunderstanding their own political systems. We assume, he says, that our countries are stable and prosperous because of democracy. But we confuse the benefits we get from democracy with those that we get from the rule of law. Pan Wei argues that democracy and the rule of law do not need to go together – in fact, like 'Ying' and 'Yang' they are in constant conflict with one another. Democracy is about giving power to the people, but the rule of law is about putting limits on that power. Democracy creates governments, but the rule of law regulates them. Democracy is about *making* laws, the rule of law about *enforcing* them. The powerbase of democracy lies in the officials we vote for – parliamentarians, ministers, prime ministers and presidents. But the power of the rule of law comes from people who are deliberately not elected – independent civil servants, judges and auditors. Where democracy draws its legitimacy from populism – elections and votes in parliament – the rule of law draws it from entrance exams and performance reviews: 'the former is about majority, and the latter about meritocracy'.

In the West, according to Pan Wei, we can enjoy both because we have reached a level of material wealth and modernity that allows the two to live side by side, balancing each other in permanent tension. On the other hand, developing countries do not have that luxury. They have to choose one or the other. Many developing countries from Yugoslavia and Rwanda to Angola and Lebanon have chosen democracy without the rule of law. The result has been chaos, as populist regimes have exploited ethnic tensions to get their hands on power. According to Pan Wei it is the premature introduction of democracy that has undermined the rule of law and modernization, forcing leaders to pander to popular sentiment rather than making painful reforms for the long term. On the other hand, Pan Wei claims, a handful of developing countries like Singapore and Hong Kong adopted the rule of law without democracy. They have known nothing but success: their economies have grown steadily, they have attracted investment, wiped out corruption and developed strong national identities.

It is no surprise that the Communist authorities are taking notice of Pan Wei's idea of 'demythologizing democracy' and separating it from the rule of law. Under his vision, a neutral civil service system would strictly and impartially enforce laws, and propose legislative bills. It would be held in permanent check by judges who would be the guardians of the Chinese Constitution. Although it is a long way from reality, Pan Wei has a vision of a high-tech consultative dictatorship, where there are no elections but decisions made by a responsive government, bound by law, and in touch with its citizens' aspirations.

Turning Western democracy on its head

The 'New Leftist', Wang Shaoguang, agrees with Pan Wei that China's senior leadership will try to pioneer a new model of politics that is the 'mirror image of the West', based on the rule of law and citizen participation rather than elections. Wang Shaoguang argues that all developed democracies are facing a political crisis: turnout in elections is falling, faith in political leaders has collapsed, parties are losing members and populism is on the rise. As they try to restore trust in the political process, Western leaders are increasingly pioneering new techniques to reach the people – going over the heads of their political parties. At a national level, referendums – like the ones held in France and Holland on the European Constitution – have heralded a return to direct democracy. At a local level, mayors and councils are increasingly organizing public hearings, conducting surveys or convening 'citizens juries' to help them make controversial decisions on issues ranging from major planning decisions to bus routes. In the West, he argues, multi-party elections are still the central part of our political process, but they have been supplemented by a vast array of these new types of deliberation.

China, he claims, will do things the other way around. The government is increasingly finding ways of involving the people in its major decisions about policy. Public consultations, expert meetings and surveys are becoming a central part of Chinese decision-making. He says that the old days when senior leaders like Mao Zedong or Deng Xiaoping would make momentous decisions alone are long gone. In the future 'deliberative democracy' will be the central part of Chinese politics, with grass-roots elections playing a supplementary rather than a central role.

This idea was described to me even more pithily by Fang Ning, a political scientist at the Chinese Academy of Social Sciences, who used a culinary metaphor. He compared democracy in the West to a fixed-menu restaurant where customers can select the identity of their chef, but have no say in what dishes he chooses to cook for them. Chinese democracy, on the other hand, always involves the same chef – the Communist Party – but the policy dishes which are served up can be chosen 'à la carte'.

Fang Ning, who first became prominent when he co-wrote *China's Road under the Shadow of Globalization* with the nationalist maverick Wang Xiaodong, has become an increasingly influential figure. He helped to draft the government's 'White Paper on Democracy' in 2005. He shares Pan Wei's opposition to elections, which he also believes would lead to the break-up of China: 'Westerners hope that elections will go up to township level, but I think that competitive elections should be restricted to villages because they are not part of the power structure.' However, this desire to restrict elections, he concedes, does put the onus on China to find other ways of legitimating its policy decisions: 'the most important question is not an independent judiciary, but that the people should have a right to participate'. When I ask him whether there are any examples of his ideas happening in practice, he points me in the direction of another political experiment that won an award from Yu Keping: 'If you want to see the future of Chinese politics,' Fang Ning says, 'go to Chongqing.'

The Chongqing experiment in participation

The undulating glass roof of Chongqing airport echoes the curve of the Wulong (Black Dragon) mountain range. Its cutting-edge design testifies to the growing affluence and ambition of this city authority. An advertising hoarding reinforces the message in pidgin English: 'Chongqing already have had the champagne flavour'. Most Western people have not even heard of it, but with 30 million citizens Chongqing is bigger than twenty-two out of the twenty-seven states of the European Union. And it is swelling by 500,000 every year. The city nestles in the hills at the confluence of the Yangtze and Jialin Jiang rivers, acting as a bridge between China's past and future. Many Chinese come here to visit 'Zhou Gong Guan', the simple house where the Communist leader Zhou En Lai and his wife settled from 1939 to 1947 in order to publish an underground newspaper and organize rebels to fight the Japanese. However, just a few minutes away is a vision of China's future. Like a cross between Rome and Manhattan, Chongqing stretches out in a forest of skyscrapers that climb up the slopes of its many hills. At night they light up to form a galaxy of red, green and yellow that radiates out from Independence Square, a monument built in 1950 to commemorate the end of the war with Japan.

Chongqing is trying to become a living laboratory for the ideas that Pan Wei, Wang Shaoguang and Fang Ning described: strengthening the rule of law and consulting the public over major decisions. Li Dianxun, the director of the city government's legal affairs office, has spearheaded the process. He is young and dynamic with a sharp suit and snappy tie. At just forty, he has been promoted twelve times in the last fourteen years, spending spells in the State Council, the government of Shanghai and at the Central Party School before settling into his current post (one of the party elders at dinner says only half in jest, 'If you come back to meet him again he will probably be running the place'). Li Dianxun has gathered around him a group of equally supercharged high-flyers: all with law degrees, some experience of living abroad and a good command of the English language.

Li Dianxun proudly tells me about his new 'freedom of information clause', and his 'regulation on accountability' which allows the local heads of government offices to be questioned and investigated if they make questionable decisions. But the most eye-catching measure that his team have introduced is the decision to make all significant government rulings subject to public hearings – in person, on television and on the internet. So far he has organized over 600 public hearings – involving 100,000 citizens – on compensation for peasants whose land has been requisitioned; on the level of the minimum wage; and on the setting of prices for public utilities like water, electricity, natural gas, roads, bridges, education, public health, public transport, sewage and refuse disposal.

The authorities are proudest of the public hearing on the price of tickets for the light railway, which saw fares reduced from 15 to just 2 Yuan. Another example was a hearing on fireworks before the last Spring Festival which overturned the blanket ban that had been introduced after a horrific accident some years earlier in favour of a licensing system. 'If the government innovations can't keep up with economic development there will be problems,' Li Dianxun claims. 'We need to give more rights and benefits to all the people; and to borrow some advanced experience from abroad.' The Chongqing experiment has attracted national attention. There have been 60,000 stories about it on websites around the country. Li Dianxun tells me that the 'senior leadership' (shorthand for President Hu Jintao, Prime Minister Wen Jiabao and the Politburo) invited him to make a presentation at the government's headquarters in Zhongnanhai. And the experiment is being emulated in other cities around China.

Chongqing is a whopper of a city. Its bewildering scale – even by China's standards 30 million inhabitants is impressive – gives its experiments with public consultation national significance. However, the real potential for public consultation – as an alternative to elections – can best be gleaned from smaller-scale experiments in the more prosperous parts of China. The most interesting one was carried out in the township of Zeguo in Wenling City, which is situated in the wealthy eastern province of Zhejiang.

What made the Zeguo consultation unique – not just in China but in the world – was the fact that it used a novel technique called 'deliberative polling' to decide on major spending decisions. This method, the brainchild of a Stanford political scientist called James Fishkin, is designed to help policy-makers consult their citizens: 'It harks back to a form of democracy quite different from modern western style party competition – Ancient Athens. In Athens, deliberative microcosms chosen by lot would make important public decisions as part of the official operations of the government.'

Deliberative polling is designed to solve a dilemma which authorities like Chongqing or Zeguo inevitably face. On the one hand, if they organize a consultation like the ones in Chongqing, only the most vocal people will turn up. They tend to represent their own interests, and are not necessarily representative of their fellow citizens. On the other hand, if Chongqing tried to consult the population directly through opinion polls, they would find that citizens knew very little about the details of particular public policy questions. As a result, they would often choose options at random, rather than ticking the 'don't know' box in a questionnaire. Deliberative polling tries to solve this conundrum by randomly selecting a sample of the population but then involving them in a consultation process with experts, before asking them to vote on their decisions. Zeguo used this technique to decide how to spend its 40 million Yuan 'public works' budget. Two hundred and seventy-five people – chosen at random – were invited to take part in a charmingly named 'democratic heart-to-heart talk'. In exchange for a free bus-pass and 50 RMB (£3.30), these citizens agreed to spend a day being briefed on the pros and cons of thirty potential building projects – from sewage plants and parks to roads and a new town square. At the end of the day, they were asked to whittle the wish-list down to twelve projects that the government could actually afford to build. Their wish-list was then presented to the local People's Congress which voted the plan through in its entirety.

So far the Zeguo experiment is a one-off, but Fishkin and the Chinese political scientist He Baogang, who advised the Zeguo government on the mechanics of the consultation, believe that 'deliberative democracy' could provide a template for political reform in China: 'it shows how governments, without party competition or the conventional institutions of representative democracy as practiced in the West, can nevertheless realize, to a high degree, two fundamental democratic values at the same time – political equality and deliberation'.

Rule of law or rule by man?

There has been less conspicuous progress on other democratic values such as freedom of expression, freedom of association, or even the one that Pan Wei has promoted so vigorously, the rule of

71

law. Over the centuries, petitions to the powerful have become a surrogate for due legal processes in China – a pattern that harks back to imperial times, but is still very much in vogue. When I walked back from my meeting with Li Dianxun in the Chongqing government offices in 2006, I stumbled upon a Mrs Wang. She was dressed in her Sunday best – a tailored jacket and skirt, shiny shoes and a touch of lipstick – because she wanted to make the right impression. She told me that she had got up early – as she does every day – to catch the officials on their way into the Chongqing Municipal Affairs Office. She was part of a small throng – all elderly and smartly dressed – that was standing opposite the building's gates. Most were former broadcasters who – after working for the party for thirty years – were laid off with only 4,000 renminbi in compensation. They were asking for more money for themselves and an 'old age foundation' to pay a fair reward to all pensioners. They clutched their tattered 'files', showing me the official stamps that signal their complaint has been lodged. Some of them had been seeking redress for four years, coming regularly to demonstrate outside the municipality's office. Mrs Wang, herself, has been to Beijing three times to present her petition to the central government. But there was no response to her or the other protesters' complaints. The authorities seemed immune to the low murmur of protest outside their offices.

Mrs Wang's demonstration was just one of the 250 demonstrations that took place in China on that very day. Statistics from the Ministry of Public Security show that these so-called 'mass incidents' – which include strikes, demonstrations, sit-ins, traffic-blocking and building seizures – have grown ten-fold in just over a decade: from 8,700 a year in 1993 to 87,000 in 2005. The numbers of demonstrators have grown too: from an average of ten protesters in the mid 1990s to over fifty today. In the first half of 2005, there were seventeen that involved more than 10,000 people. Not all of them were peaceful and good-natured. In the first half of 2005, 1,700 people were injured and 100 killed in these organized demonstrations. All of the demonstrations are triggered by feelings of injustice: for better working conditions, unpaid wages and pensions, and compensation. A report from the Chinese Academy of Social Sciences showed that 40 million peasants had had their land confiscated to build airports, roads, dams, factories and for private land deals. Every year, a further 2 million people will lose their homes and lands to make way for new developments (in deals that often see local party bosses lining their pockets at their expense).

In a country whose political system is ruled according to the whims of party officials, these incidents are too often resolved on the streets. However, it is the fear of instability that is leading the theorists of 'deliberative dictatorship' to look beyond the system of petitioning which Chinese people have used to vent their grievances since imperial times. Pan Wei urges China to trade its corrupt and unpredictable 'rule by man' for the 'rule of law'. He hopes that China will do this by separating politics from government and establishing a truly independent civil service, judiciary and anti-corruption agency. But when pressed how these revolutionary changes could happen, Pan Wei is much less sure-footed.

There is still a long way for China to go before it develops the rule of law – and Pan Wei's vision will certainly not be realized so long as the Communist Party remains above the law. However, Pan Wei can point to some progress. China is one of the only one-party states to allow citizens to sue the state in court. The number of law suits of citizens against the government has increased from 10,000 five years ago to 100,000 last year. And the rate at which citizens win cases against the government has also changed dramatically –

from single digits to over 40 per cent. According to Pan Wei, the quality of the proceedings is slowly improving: 'Fifteen years ago most of the judges were retired officials or military officers. Today they all have legal training.'

The government seems to realize that developing institutional ways of dealing with grievances can make the state more stable. If there is a system of legal redress, citizens can be compensated for ills rather than punished for dissent. This is in line with the authorities' so-called 'flexible approach' of conceding legitimate complaints from ordinary people, while punishing the ring-leaders. The senior leadership has already intervened several times in high-profile cases. For example, in April 2005, Prime Minister Wen Jiabao personally intervened to stop the construction of a dam in the Nujiang River; in Zhejiang, workers were allowed to negotiate collectively with their employers; in Yinchuan, a cab strike ended with an unusual compromise with the government. So far, the protests have been isolated local events – and President Hu Jintao and Prime Minister Wen Jiabao have managed to deflect criticism on to 'corrupt local authorities', thereby allowing themselves to take the side of the 'little guy'. But this may prove more challenging in the long run.

Whose rule of law?

The debate about political reform – like the one about economics – sometimes pits the 'New Left' against the 'New Right'. Although some members of the 'New Right' are convinced democrats, many are more focused on promoting the rule of law, to reduce the size of the state and restrict its impact on the market. On the Left there is more support for elections as a way of endowing the government with enough legitimacy to take on vested interests and redistribute wealth. They fear deliberative dictatorship would lead to an impoverished, consumerist model of politics.

The 'New Leftist' Wang Hui argues that it will be impossible to develop the 'New Left' agenda without wider political reform, because China's new rich have a stranglehold on politics. 'You need democracy in order to empower the state to take money from special interests to pay for public goods. In the 1990s there was a dichotomy between a free market and an authoritarian state. People thought that the economic reforms were working and that we could reform the state later. Now we see that many of the problems we are facing are a product of economic reforms and we need political reform to correct them.'

Pan Wei, whose political sympathies are closer to the 'New Right', admits that his attachment to the 'rule of law' reflects his pro-market agenda: 'democracy is rooted in the belief in the eventual election of "good" leaders... rule of law is rooted in the disbelief of "persons", it trusts no one who holds power'. The central feature of Pan Wei's model, therefore, would be a very small government. Its main role would be enforcing rather than producing laws, because the checks and balances would deliberately make it very hard to pass any laws.

Wang Hui, on the other hand, argues that the 'rule of law' is meaningless without democracy. Every year, he says, the people's congresses pass hundreds of laws that have no impact at all: 'We are all for the rule of law,' he says, 'but whose laws will be listened to? Compare labour law and intellectual property. Both laws have been on the table for a decade, but on labour law nothing has happened, while on intellectual property everything is happening. Without popular participation, only the interests of capital will be listened to.' In fact, it is precisely because the affluent middle classes fear their assets could be appropriated by the masses that they are lukewarm about democracy.

Science and democracy

Many observers talk about Chinese politics as if it had been kept in the deep freeze for the last thirty years, while everything else changed around it. In fact, China's politics has changed almost as much as the economy – just not in a direction that the West is comfortable with. What has emerged in the place of the liberal democracy that the West predicted is a more sophisticated variant of dictatorship.

Wang Shaoguang argues that Chinese politics is almost unrecognizable from the Mao Zedong and Deng Xiaoping eras. The age of 'strong men politics' where rulers would take decisions on their own has given way to a style of policy-making that is remarkably open to the influences of experts, the media, and even public opinion (usually mediated through opinion polls). For example, Prime Minister Wen Jiabao commissioned research from over 100 academic institutions for his 11th Five Year Plan – involving officials from every branch of central and local government. The Communist Party's favourite terms for this new style are 'scientific' and 'democratic', but in the West we would probably call it 'technocratic' because it empowers technical experts rather than the public or political leaders.

Few of these changes have been noted by Western observers. Wang Shaoguang says: 'the analytical framework of authoritarianism from the West is completely unable to capture these deep changes in Chinese politics. In the past several decades, this label has been casually put on China from the late Qing era to the early years of the Republic, the eras of warlords, Jiang Jieshi, Mao Zedong, Deng Xiaoping and Jiang Zemin. Chinese politics has made world-shaking changes during this period, but the label put on it made no change at all.'

The reason that few Westerners have acknowledged the changes to China's political system is that the reforms have been geared towards preserving the one-party state, rather than embracing liberal democracy. Western theorists tend to fall back on well-worked-out theories to explain why China's democratization is inevitable. Some say that it will be democratic when its GDP per capita reaches $5,000. Others think that the rise of its middle class will make democracy irresistible. Others again – such as Will Hutton – say that the functional needs of an advanced modern economy (freedom of inquiry, free flow of information, rule of law) will soon make China have to choose between going bust or becoming democratic. Finally there is the school of thought that the rise of civil society will bring political liberalization in its wake.

These theories may well prove to be correct in the long term, but the assumption that political change can only lead in one direction has blinded many observers to the remarkable political changes that China has already implemented. After three decades of reform, China has made steady improvements in developing the rule of law and professionalizing its civil service but it has developed very few of the tenets of liberal democracy. With remarkable ease, the Chinese authorities have been able to co-opt each political reform to entrench the power of the ruling Communist Party.

Nowhere is this truer than when it comes to the internet. The internet was one of the forces guaranteed to change China. However, in the event it is China that has changed the internet: forcing internet giants like Google, Microsoft and Yahoo to play by its rules. Most dictatorships see the internet as akin to the weather. You can cover yourself when it rains, but you cannot control the seasons. For example, the Zimbabwean leader Robert Mugabe shuts down domestic websites when they criticize the government – the equivalent of opening an umbrella – but his crude intimidation does not change the flow of information in and out of the country. Burma, Iran, Vietnam and Tunisia have tried to build a wall around their countries, but their protection is more like a sieve than a barrier. Saudi Arabia has had more success, bringing all traffic on to a single internet provider and screening out sites that offend its clerics with a web-link that describes the content as 'un-Islamic'. China is sixty times the size of Saudi Arabia, and most experts agreed that the sheer volume of traffic would be impossible to police. However, Beijing has risen to the challenge, throwing people, money and technology at the problem. The more lurid accounts talk of an e-police force of 100,000 people employed to scour the net, blocking sites and checking e-mails. The numbers are probably exaggerated, but analysts agree that teams of computer scientists run a firewall with at least four different kinds of filter.

Much of the commentary about this censorship suggests that China is an iron-clad Stalinist state, shielded from global events by the 'great firewall of China'. However, analogies with Russia and Eastern Europe in the 1980s are misleading. The governments of the Soviet bloc looked on powerlessly as their grey world of prop-aganda was eclipsed by Technicolor images of a better life in the West. China, on the other hand, is already part of the capitalist world. It is awash with information, products and all the baubles of consumer society. With every year that passes, the number of people with access to these goodies grows.

China's interference is very tightly targeted on issues that could undermine the regime. Internet providers mainly censor the perennial political taboos: articles on Tibet, Taiwan, Tiananmen Square and the Falun Gong religious sect as well as pieces criticiz-ing the Communist Party's rule. This kind of censorship is not aimed at shutting China off from the world, but rather at zeroing in on political controversy. Google, for example, estimates that less than 2 per cent of internet searches will be affected by censorship.

The authorities are less worried about information coming in from outside than they are about Chinese people talking to one another. China's laws on the freedom of assembly are draconian. Charities, trade unions and religious groups are kept under close surveillance and regularly banned. The ferocity with which the Communist Party suppresses the herbivorous and mild-mannered Falun Gong has puzzled many outside observers. But Beijing is not afraid of the content of their meetings; it is afraid of them meeting at all. China's history of revolutions organized by secret societies and religious sects has taught the government to be careful. Its greatest fear is that, in a country where political gatherings are restricted, the net could provide a virtual meeting place for the masses to organize.

The great firewall is full of leaks. For example, when the dissident blogger Michael Anti's site was shut down, its content was copied and distributed across the net. Many Chinese take refuge in the world of digital images, which can be sent between mobiles or e-mailed as attachments, escaping the filters of the censor. Others write to each other in coded language using stories as allegories on message boards. But so far the government has been adept at keeping up with technology – and using it to advance its own agenda.

Is deliberative dictatorship a real alternative?

The big questions are whether the Communist Party can continue adapting, and whether deliberative dictatorship can prove a robust alternative to liberal democracy? Certainly, the authorities seem willing to experiment with all kinds of political innovations. In

Pingchang, they have been willing to introduce greater democracy within the party. In Chongqing, they have given up a certain amount of judicial power and allowed public voices to be heard. In Zeguo, they have introduced a form of government by focus group. The main criterion guiding political reform seems to be that it must not threaten the Communist Party's monopoly on power. You could call it 'Anything but National Elections'.

Can a more responsive form of authoritarianism evolve into a legitimate and stable form of government? The reason that the Soviet planned economy collapsed is that its planners were unable to gather enough information to allocate resources efficiently, and motivate people to maximize the creation of wealth. The conventional wisdom is that as societies become more complex, with more and more interest groups clashing with each other, the planned political system will suffer from the same inefficiencies. But could new technology give leaders access to perfect information? It is possible to imagine that polling, internet consultations and public hearings could allow the authorities in Beijing to keep abreast of the public mood.

As China becomes more complex – and the interests of the poor clash with those of the new rich; urban dwellers with those of the countryside; shareholders with employees – it will be impossible to please all of the people all of the time. In these circumstances it will not be enough to make the right decisions – governments need to be seen to have made them in a legitimate way so that the losers accept them as well as the winners. Elections can give that legitimacy because everyone takes part in them. However, will deliberative polls such as the one in Zeguo (where only 275 people out of 120,000 citizens take part) be seen as legitimate?

In the long term, China's one-party state may well collapse. However, in the medium term, the regime seems to be developing increasingly sophisticated techniques to prolong its survival and pre-empt discontent. One of the reasons why it seems to be so resilient is its mixture of pragmatism and responsiveness. The Chinese government is, in some ways, its own sternest critic. It constantly commissions and researches its own vulnerabilities. In fact, whenever Western scholars write reports on the impending collapse of China's one-party state they seem to draw on studies commissioned by the state itself. And when the Communist regime looks for mechanisms to entrench its power, it takes as much inspiration from the practices of advanced democracies as other autocracies. China has already changed the terms of the debate about globalization by proving that authoritarian regimes can deliver economic growth. In the future, its model of deliberative dictatorship could prove that one-party states can deliver stability as well.

CHAPTER THREE

Comprehensive National Power

> The Rise of China is granted by nature. In the last 2,000 years
> China has enjoyed superpower status several times . . . Even as
> recently as 1820, just 20 years before the Opium War, China
> accounted for 30% of world GDP. This history of superpower
> status makes the Chinese people very proud of their country
> on the one hand, and on the other hand very sad about China's
> current international status. They believe China's decline to be a
> historical mistake which they should correct.
>
> Yan Xuetong, 'The Rise of China in Chinese Eyes'

In the shadow of the iconic Summer Palace, in a north-west
suburb of Beijing, lies the Central Party School of the Communist
Party. This inner sanctum – which was run by Hu Jintao until he
ascended to the Presidency in 2002 – is filled with official ideo-
logues who act as custodians of the party's doctrine, passing on
their wisdom to future leaders.

Before they are promoted all cadres must complete a course
at the school – typically lasting 100 days – designed to recharge
their ideological batteries. The school is a typically Chinese mix of
the grandiose and the mundane, set out like a utopian socialist
commune with wide tree-lined avenues and ceremonial buildings

sitting alongside high-rise apartment blocks with clothes lines hanging from their balconies.

In early 2005 I found myself sitting inside one of its training rooms, surrounded by some of China's brightest and best foreign policy thinkers, watching a PowerPoint presentation on China's power by the 'New Leftist' economist Hu Angang. It is common-place for China's porous government to bring together thinkers to discuss policy and strategy. But what was unusual about this event was the fact that the organizers decided, apparently for the first time in the school's history, to invite some foreign policy experts from abroad. And so it was that I, along with half a dozen hand-picked 'international scholars', made the journey to the CCCPS. Under a huge blue banner reading 'China and the world: power, role and strategy', Li Junru, the vice-chairman of the school and an erudite interpreter of party dogma, opened the discussion with a flourish: 'the Central Party School is regarded as mysterious, but today it is open to the whole world. This will be recorded as an important moment in our history.'

Comprehensive National Power

China must be the most self-aware rising power in history. It is hard to imagine advisers to Napoleon, Lord Palmerston, Bismarck, or even George Bush drawing up complex charts to rank their own country's economic, political and military power against the competition. But that is precisely what Hu Angang was trying to do in our seminar. And he is by no means alone. Measuring 'CNP' – short for Comprehensive National Power – has become a national obsession.

'CNP' is more than a cute acronym for Chinese strategists. From the time of Sun Zi onwards, the Chinese have concluded that it is only by looking at your opponent's weaknesses that you can understand your own strengths.

Each of the major foreign policy think-tanks has devised its own index to give a numerical value to every nation's power. The Chinese Academy of Social Sciences (CASS) was first to pioneer the approach – devising an index with sixty-four indicators of power in 1996. Not to be outdone the Chinese Institute for Contemporary International Relations – a vast think-tank banked by China's spooks at the State Security Ministry – developed a rival toolkit, using 'expert surveys, regression analysis, nerve networks and cluster analysis'. In 1999, the military also joined the party, commissioning the Chinese Military Academy to develop its own seemingly scientific formula for measuring national power ($P = K \times H \times S$).

In this era of globalization and universal norms, it is striking that Chinese strategists have an unashamed focus on 'national' power. The idea of recapturing sovereignty from global economic forces, companies and groups of individuals such as terrorists is a potentially revolutionary element of the Chinese world-view.

However, perhaps it is the idea of being 'comprehensive' that is most distinctively Chinese. All of the CNP indexes stress political and economic as well as military power. And more recently there have been attempts to find ways of measuring that most intangible form of power – cultural attraction. One academic explains why comprehensiveness is the key to power with an analogy from the past. 'Why,' Professor Yan Xuetong asks, 'was the Soviet Union so much more powerful than Japan in the 1980s?' He points out that in 1985 the Soviet Union's GDP was only $741.9 billion compared to Japan's $1,220 billion. But while Japan was an economic lion, it was a military mouse. The impoverished Soviet Union, on the other hand, had a military machine that was on a par with the USA's. 'Thus,' he argues, 'the comprehensive power of the Soviet Union was of the superpower-level, while Japan was merely a major power.'

The conclusion is clear: in the same way that balanced development is the holy grail of reformers in domestic policy, so too is it vital for China to have what Chinese academics call a 'balanced power-profile'. The Ying of economic power must be balanced with the Yang of military, political and moral heft.

Even with their complex methodologies for measuring power, Chinese researchers are struggling to keep up with their country's rapid growth. In the league-tables of the 1990s, Beijing languished behind the USA, Japan, Russia and several European countries. However according to the latest calculations on all the different indexes, China has eclipsed them all bar the USA. The curious thing is that the more power their country accumulates, the more cautious its foreign policy thinkers become about flaunting it.

Nourishing obscurity

In Bertolt Brecht's play, *Galileo*, the eponymous astronomer was free to expound on all of his celestial discoveries, except the most important one: the fact that the earth moves round the sun. For almost a generation, Chinese foreign policy makers have suffered a similar predicament: the one topic that has been off-bounds is China's ascent to great power status. The Chinese phrase for 'rise', '*jueqi*', became a virtual taboo.

Chinese officials were terrified that the rest of the world would see China's rise as a threat, and therefore gang up against it. They hoped that if they refused to talk about their country's rise, the rest of the world might not notice it was happening. They preferred instead to talk of 'development', a political euphemism which, in

Orwell's words, would allow them 'to name things without calling up mental pictures of them'.

China's seemingly inexorable 'development' has been guided by a slogan of Deng Xiaoping's, the injunction to '*tao guang yang hui*', which literally means to 'hide brightness, nourish obscurity'. When he first coined the phrase – officially translated as 'bide our time and build our capabilities' – Deng Xiaoping meant that China, as a poor and weak country, should avoid conflicts and concentrate on economic development. In the same way that he had abandoned Mao's commitment to central planning in domestic policy, Deng Xiaoping quietly jettisoned China's revolutionary foreign policy of supporting Communist 'fifth columns' in South-East Asian countries; fighting wars with India and Vietnam; and regarding multilateral institutions with suspicion.

Deng Xiaoping's new strategy, of not having a visible foreign policy, meant that China should stay neutral in wars, conflicts about spheres of influence or struggles over natural resources – or as he said, 'don't stick your head out'. In order to do this, Beijing should be humble and 'yield on small issues with the long term in mind'. And it should abandon its Cold War habit of only making friends with other socialist countries. From now on China should open its arms to any country that could assist in its quest for markets, natural resources and political support.

For American strategists like Paul Wolfowitz, Robert Kagan or John Mearsheimer, looking for evidence of a 'China threat', the behaviour of the People's Republic can be bewildering. Although they claim that China is looking for a 'place in the sun' like rising powers past, Beijing seems intent on undermining their claims. Rather than mimicking the bellicose behaviour of Germany under Kaiser Wilhelm or Imperial Japan, China seems obsessed with avoiding conflict.

The inspiration for this approach is as old as the hills. From the days of Sun Zi's 'Art of War', Chinese thinkers have regarded war as a failure of strategy, preferring to manipulate situations so that they can get their way without a single shot being fired. But if its goals are ancient, the content of China's grand strategy is very modern. Many of the most sophisticated and progressive-sounding ideas in Western strategic thinking have been put to use by Chinese thinkers.

They have discovered that nourishing obscurity is a difficult business, particularly if your country has the largest population in the world, your economy is growing at 10 per cent a year, your defence budgets are growing even faster, and your companies are investing all over the world. In China's universities and think-tanks, a growing clamour of thinkers called for Deng Xiaoping's approach to be scrapped. By the end of 2003 the pressure became irresistible.

The fall of the 'Peaceful Rise'

There could not have been a prettier place to break the taboo on China's rise. Hainan Island, with its straw-hatted peasants, water buffaloes and paddy fields, is the kind of pre-modern paradise that Westerners associate with traditional China. Its most glamorous resort, in the town of Bo'ao, stretches out in an archipelago of luxury hotels with palm trees, landscaped gardens, swimming pools disguised as rock pools, and golf courses so perfect that they look like computer animations. It was here – in front of an invited audience that included George Bush Snr and a string of global leaders near if not quite at the top of world politics – that the Orwellian-sounding 'Peaceful Rise of China' was first launched.

Zheng Bijian, who coined the phrase, has been a sort of intellectual ambassador for China's leaders since the late 1970s, when at Deng Xiaoping's request he travelled to the West as part of a group of scholars. As a former vice-chair of the elite Central Party School (when the President of China, Hu Jintao, was its chairman) and a one-time minister for propaganda he is well connected. But it is nevertheless almost unprecedented for a figure outside the government to launch a major new concept on its behalf.

On one of his trips to the USA, Zheng Bijian had been struck by how many people saw China's rise as a threat. Staying silent, he argued, was doing little to defuse these fears. China should get on the front foot and explain its development to the world.

'China's rise,' he said at the beginning of the Bo'ao Forum, 'is an entirely new phenomenon unseen in world history.' Warming to his theme he explained that 'China will not take the road of Germany of World War I, or Germany and Japan World War II – using violence to pillage resources and seek world hegemony.' Unlike the former Soviet Union whose development was cut off from the rest of the world, China would be integrated into economic globalization, providing markets, and economic opportunities for the rest of the world. And, unlike the USA, he claimed, China will not seek to become a 'hegemonic power' by building alliances like NATO that are directed against other countries. In a direct reply to Kagan, Wolfowitz and Mearsheimer, he claimed that China's rise will create a 'win-win' situation for the world, spreading peace and prosperity in its wake.

Zheng Bijian's idea is supported by a growing group of 'liberal internationalists' in China. These thinkers – such as Qin Yaqing and Shi Yinhong – believe that China should abandon its victim complex and play a more active role in international affairs. The starting point has to be an acknowledgement that China is rising. But in parallel with this admission, Beijing must have a concerted strategy to show that China is interested in joining rather than overthrowing the existing international order. They want China to become more assertive in defending its interests, but to do so within the existing system. Zheng Bijian's theory was not made up as he went along. He had prevailed upon his former colleague at the Central Party School, President Hu Jintao, to finance a major research project – largely carried out by PhD students from Shanghai – that looked at forty case studies of rising powers. Their consensus was that rising powers 'which chose the road of aggression and expansion' have ultimately failed.

The theory of 'Peaceful Rise' immediately provoked a counter-attack from the assertive nationalists in Beijing's universities. They are China's neo-cons, or considering their formal affiliation, 'neo-comms'. One of the most vocal is Professor Yan Xuetong, Director of the Institute of International Studies at Tsinghua University. 'Peaceful Rise is wrong,' he told me in his Beijing office, 'because it gives Taiwan a message that they can declare independence and we will not attack them.' Yan Xuetong, like many Chinese strategists, argues that no great nation in history ever rose in peace. While he thinks that China should do all it can to avoid war, he fears that one with Taiwan is probably inevitable if Beijing does not abandon its goal of reunification. He is angry at the influence that liberal internationalists have had on Chinese foreign policy: 'The basic difference between us and them is that they emphasize appease-ment and we want containment,' he says. 'This applies to the USA, Japan and Taiwan. Their basic argument is that because China is weak we should make concessions. We think that if you make con-cessions, they will just ask for more. The problems we are having with Japan and Taiwan are a direct result of years of appeasement.'

When I tell him that he has been labelled a Chinese neo-con, he does not demur: 'I do not feel very angry about being called a Chinese neo-con, but I prefer to be called a "realist".' The 'neo-comm' label will stick because there are so many parallels between

Yan Xuetong and his analogues in the USA. Yan Xuetong is almost the mirror image of William Kristol, the editor of the Washington-based *Weekly Standard* and founder of the 'educational' Project for the New American Century. Where Kristol is obsessed with a China threat and convinced that US supremacy is the only solution for a peaceful world order, Yan Xuetong is fixated with the USA and sure that China's military modernization is the key to world stability. Like Kristol, he is a keen admirer of Churchill. Like Kristol, he presents himself as a lone voice in the wilderness. Like Kristol he is media savvy – propagating his ideas through magazines such as *World Affairs* and *Global Times* and tapping into a deep seam of popular nationalism.

The swing-voters in this battle of wills are the largest group in Chinese foreign policy: the pragmatists. They were largely unimpressed by the 'Peaceful Rise', pointing to its failure to offer either a comprehensive grand strategy or a reassuring narrative to the world. Wang Jisi, one of the most respected and articulate thinkers on Chinese foreign policy, declared that the idea was still half-baked and needed more work before being adopted. He attacked the theory's failure to say anything about political reform at home or global governance abroad. At the same time, many pragmatists think that 'Peaceful Rise' fails to reassure the world. They remain opposed to talking about China's rise, fearing that it will fan rather than defuse the idea of a China threat. According to them, China's best strategy is to be modest about the extent of its power, in order to concentrate on economic growth and social development. They think that the government should stick to phrases such as development, which are 'bloodless, less aggressive and much less controversial'.

For a short while the 'Peaceful Rise' caught on. China's president and prime minister used the phrase in public speeches in late 2003 and early 2004, setting off on a tour of Asia to preach its gospel. Then the backlash began. The Ministry of Foreign Affairs, aggrieved that it had been excluded from developing the concept, poured cold water on it. And Jiang Zemin, the former president whose 'Shanghai Gang' are in favour of a more assertive foreign policy, used an attack on the term as a means of re-establishing their own influence.

The 'Peaceful Rise' did not survive these bitter wrangles. When the bureaucratic in-fighting took off, Hu Jintao and Wen Jiabao quietly dropped the phrase, reverting to the Deng-era concept of 'Peace and Development'. Zheng Bijian himself, in an attempt to keep his concept alive, began to qualify his thesis so much that it was eviscerated of much of its content. In later speeches he explained that force was justified to protect Chinese sovereignty, stop Taiwanese independence, and even to get exploitable oil and gas reserves. But although the term has lost its official endorsement, the remarkable debate which the phrase provoked is continuing to rage. The liberal internationalists, who want China to join the Western world and fight for its rights within the system, are continuing to struggle with the neo-comms whose long-term goal is to build an alternative system with China in its centre. And in the middle are the pragmatists who will support any idea that advances China's interests. All three camps are mixing Western theories with traditional Chinese thinking to advance their cause.

They have taken three of the most striking Western ideas about globalization and turned them on their head, transforming concepts used to describe the decline of the nation state into strategies for increasing China's national power. For example, the idea of 'soft power', which is associated in the West with the attractiveness of companies such as McDonald's and Levi's, has been transformed in Chinese hands into a quest by the Chinese state to recapture the 'moral high-ground' of international relations. The idea of 'multilateralism' is associated in the West with the dilution of national sovereignty as member states agree to be bound by the rules of supranational institutions like the European Union or World Trade Organization. It has been recast as a tool of national power projection that allows China to develop links with other Asian countries that exclude the USA. Finally the idea of 'asymmetric war' – coined to describe the tactics of guerrilla groups such as the Viet Cong or al-Qaeda – has been rethought by China on an industrial scale. Chinese strategists have explored ways of using military weapons, financial assets and international law to challenge US power rather than seeking to match its might in conventional terms. As the discussion below shows, Chinese liberal internationalists and neo-comms alike are pushing against the barriers of Deng Xiaoping's foreign policy orthodoxy to promote the idea of a 'Walled World'.

Soft power

Yang Yi is a military man, a rear admiral in the navy and the head of China's leading military think-tank. But his ideas on power go far beyond assessments of the latest weapons systems. He argues that the USA has created a 'strategic siege' around China by assuming the 'moral height' in international relations. Every time the People's Republic tries to assert itself in diplomatic terms, to modernize its military or to open relationships with other countries, the USA presents it as a threat. And the rest of the world, Yang Yi complains, all too often takes its lead from the hyper-power. According to him 'the United States has the final say on making and revising the international rules of the game. They have dominated international discourse, occupying the "moral highground" of the majority of international public opinions and rules of conduct. Therefore, what often occurs in international affairs is that the United States argues "only we can do this, and you can't do this".

Chinese thinkers are desperately trying to free themselves from this trap. One of the hottest buzz-words in Chinese foreign policy circles is '*ruan quanli*' – the Chinese term for 'soft power'. This modish concept was invented by the American political scientist Joseph Nye in 1990, but it is being promoted with far more zeal in Beijing than in Washington DC. Unlike its more aggressive antithesis 'hard power', which is about bribing or forcing other countries to do what you want, 'soft power' is defined as the ability to get others to want what you want. It depends neither on economic carrots nor political sticks, but rather on the attractiveness of your culture and ideas, your legitimacy in the eyes of others, and your ability to set the rules in international organizations.

Chinese scholars, such as Yang Yi and Yan Xuetong, complain that for most of the last twenty years 'soft power' has been the preserve of the West: Western countries had the biggest markets; Western culture and morality were the most aspirational; and the international institutions created after the Second World War were also Western constructs, with membership open to the rest of the world only if they met certain standards of behaviour. But now they are planning to change all that. As Yan Xuetong explains, 'during a period of globalization the sphere of competition is no longer about land, resources or markets but rule-making, setting regulations, norms or customs. After the cold war these rules are changing. Rather than being passive recipients of these changes, we should join the competition to set the global rules.'

The starting point has been to study the USA. Chinese thinkers have studied the way that Uncle Sam came to symbolize freedom and affluence, how the Statue of Liberty, the Bill of Rights,

Coca-Cola, McDonald's, CNN and Hollywood became far more effective ambassadors for the American world-view than anyone in the State Department. They looked at how American values were enshrined in a series of global institutions, such as NATO, the World Bank and the IMF, which embodied and reinforced the American way of doing things. And they noted how the large number of foreign students at American universities, the ubiquity of American companies and the power of American news services has amplified the transmission of American perspectives on global issues.

China has begun to emulate these techniques. Its Education Ministry will set up 100 'Confucius Institutes' to teach Chinese and promote Chinese culture, in the same way that the British Council and Goethe-Institut do for European culture (it has already set up thirty-two in twenty-three countries). China's international TV station – the sinister-sounding CCTV 9 – is designed to grow into a global news station to rival CNN. Beijing has expanded and professionalized the party-controlled news-wire Xinhua in the hope that it will be taken as seriously as Reuters or AP. It plans to quadruple the number of foreigners learning Chinese – to 100 million – by 2010. It has opened its universities to foreign students, attracting twice as many students from Indonesia as the USA every year and 13,000 from South Korea.

The most interesting aspect of China's 'soft power' agenda is the message they are promoting to the world. In April 2006, a conference was organized in Beijing to launch the 'China Dream'. Zheng Bijian was back with a new idea, heading a high-powered cast of speakers – including government ministers, academics and diplomats – that saw 'cultural rejuvenation' as a way of getting greater legitimacy on the world stage. The 'China Dream' they offered to the world was an attempt to associate the People's

Republic with three powerful ideas: economic development, political sovereignty and international law.

China has become both a model and a champion for the world's poorest countries, in the process fundamentally changing the way that many think about development. In 1989, Francis Fukuyama argued in a famous essay that 'What we may be witnessing is not just the end of the Cold War . . . but the end of history as such: that is, the end point of mankind's ideological evolution and the universalization of Western liberal democracy as the final form of human government.' And for the next decade, it was hard to disagree that economic and political liberalization were two sides of a seamless whole. But China's rise – and its ability to combine a gradual opening of the economy, a large state sector and authoritarian rule – has broken the link. In developing countries – in Africa, the Middle East and Central Asia – elites argue that they should follow the Chinese model of pursuing economic reforms first and political reforms later. And for the first time in a generation, some of their citizens actually believe them. It is no longer axiomatic that liberal democracy is the necessary foundation for development.

China has sought to contrast its belief in the sovereignty and the right of countries to be free from intervention in their internal affairs with the Western penchant for humanitarian intervention. China has been offering political support, economic aid and weapons to regimes that might otherwise be susceptible to international pressure, including Sudan, Iran, Burma, Zimbabwe, North Korea, Uzbekistan, Kazakhstan and Angola. Its December 2005 Africa White Paper says it will offer aid with no conditions attached. Beijing has removed all tariffs on trade for forty-five underdeveloped countries. It runs trade deficits with its neighbours in South-East Asia and it has massively increased its Overseas Development Assistance (in 2004 it gave away $1.5 billion to Asia and \$2.7 billion to Africa). The way that China disperses its aid and political support is central to the People's Republic's appeal. Where Western donors increasingly tie their aid to demands for the protection of human rights and political reform, Beijing is avowedly non-judgemental about political behaviour in its dealings with Third World countries. It applies only one criterion to the relationship: does it serve China's interests? Although China has been happy to support autocratic regimes, it does not want to become the head of a coalition of failing ones. When China's relationship with regimes in North Korea, Sudan, Zimbabwe and Burma threatened to become an embarrassment, Beijing encouraged them to take steps to become more acceptable to the international community, thereby reducing the chances that the West would take coercive action against them.

Finally, Chinese scholars have noted that the legitimacy of the USA's global leadership has been enhanced by the openness of a political system that gives other nations a chance to have their views heard in the battles between the State Department, Pentagon and the White House. However, in recent years many countries have complained of US arrogance as they have struggled to influence the lonely superpower's decisions. China has taken note and developed a brand of 'listening diplomacy', contrasting its multilateralism with America's unilateralism. As Yan Xuetong argues, 'in the next 10 years, its hegemonic position will drive the United States to continue its unilateralist foreign policy. Meanwhile, China will maintain its multilateral diplomacy to harmonize relationships with her neighbours, the EU and the developing countries of other regions.' He continues optimistically, 'thus they may even forge a strategic alliance against the United States'.

Western observers are sceptical about the extent to which China has acquired soft power, pointing out that few liberal democracies would trade their freedom for China's Communist market economy. Green tea, Jackie Chan and Confucius, they argue, are no match for McDonald's, Hollywood and the Gettysburg Address. However, China has managed to associate itself with a number of big ideas that are potentially very attractive to middle-income and developing countries, particularly those which have been subject to Western colonialism (in other words, 90 per cent of the world's countries). And because China is the largest country to champion these ideas, it can draw a lot of legitimacy from them.

It is hard to argue that China's soft power has not been on an upward curve. Part of the reason is that China started from a very low base. To its neighbours it had been a menace during the Mao years, fomenting revolution and instability in the region. And to the rest of the world it had been a stranger: unaligned and uninterested for many decades. The combination of skilful diplomacy and the lustre of thirty years of double-digit growth has allowed China to turn these perceptions around. A recent BBC World Service poll showed that China's influence in the world was seen as positive by a majority or plurality of citizens in fourteen out of the twenty-two countries that were surveyed (in total 48 per cent saw China's influence as positive – 10 per cent higher than the USA).

In the long term, as some Chinese scholars recognize, Beijing will struggle to achieve global legitimacy without substantial changes at home. Yan Xuetong puts it well: 'If you do not have a good political system at home, you cannot attract support from your neighbors. If China wants to increase its soft power, it must have political reform.' But in the medium term, China is likely to be the primary beneficiary of the fall in American soft power after the Iraq War, basing its popularity on an attempt to be seen as America's mirror image. Where American policy-makers champion the Washington Consensus, the Chinese talk about the success of gradualism and the 'Harmonious Society'. Where the USA is bellicose, Chinese policy-makers talk about peace. Whereas American diplomats talk about regime change, their Chinese counterparts talk about respect for sovereignty and the diversity of civilizations. Whereas American foreign policy uses sanctions and isolation to back up its political objectives, the Chinese offer aid and trade with no strings attached. Whereas America imposes its preferences on reluctant allies, China makes a virtue of listening to countries from around the world. Against this backdrop, Chinese diplomats and statesmen have discovered that '80 per cent of success,' as Woody Allen said, 'is just showing up.'

Multilateral power projection

Six months after the collapse of the Soviet Union, thirty-four of America's brightest foreign policy strategists gathered at Stanford University to develop 'a new organizing principle for thinking about the world and how to act in it'. Their hope was to replace George Kennan's Cold War doctrine of containment and deterrence with a new philosophy for a post-Cold War world. Out went old concepts like the imperative of military build-up, the balance of power, the spying and secrecy of the Cold War. In their place, a new big idea: building a regime of 'co-operative security' that would allow all countries to benefit from a peace dividend. Unlike alliances such as NATO, which were aimed at a single opponent, 'co-operative security' would be about building trust between nations through transparency and mutual surveillance.

As the idea gained greater currency, it caught the eye of Yan Xuetong. He told me that he was excited by 'the novelty of the idea that military co-operation does not need to be aimed against another power (unlike NATO which was set up against Russia). That makes it less threatening.' He began to wonder if co-operative security could provide a mechanism for China to modernize and build up its military without attracting the suspicion of its neighbours – precisely the opposite of what the concept's original authors had in mind. At this stage he was working as a researcher at the Chinese Institute of Contemporary International Relations – the think-tank affiliated to the State Security Ministry – and he assembled a group to refine the concept. Their work led to a body of ideas that would eventually come to be known as the 'New Security Concept'.

The 'New Security Concept' makes a distinction between 'traditional' security threats (the danger of invasion by other countries) and 'non-traditional' ones (terrorism, secessionism, environmental destruction, pandemics). Yan Xuetong correctly believed that the military alliances of the future could be arranged around these inchoate 'non-traditional threats' – bringing states together against abstract nouns such as 'terrorism' rather than hostile nations. Behind Yan Xuetong's 'New Security Concept' was a strong impulse that China should abandon its hostility to multilateral institutions. China was starting to benefit from globalization and preparing to join the World Trade Organization. And Yan Xuetong argued that it should be possible to recast the relationship with China's neighbours around similar institutions. It was not long before Yan Xuetong's theory became a reality.

The first move was towards China's western neighbours. Four years after the end of the Soviet Union, China came together with Russia, Kazakhstan, Kyrgyzstan and Tajikistan to develop a 'co-operative security arrangement' called the 'Shanghai Five'. They started by negotiating treaties demilitarizing the 4,300-mile border that they share and gradually expanded their co-operation to include security and trade. In 2001 Uzbekistan joined, and they turned this nascent grouping into the 'Shanghai Co-operation Organization' (SCO). The new organization has already established a 'regional anti-terrorism structure' in Uzbekistan, a 'business council' in Moscow and a permanent secretariat in Beijing. It has organized co-operation on economic, border and law enforcement matters, as well as two combined military exercises. India, Pakistan, Mongolia and Iran have all joined the SCO as observers. The USA is rightly concerned about this development: if at some point the observers joined as full members, the SCO would boast four nuclear states, three major economies and vast energy resources.

The Shanghai Co-operation Organization is unique. It gives the lie to the idea that only Western countries can establish successful multilateral organizations. It bears the name of a Chinese city. The values it enshrines are those of the Chinese state. Although there are differences of emphasis between Beijing and Moscow, with Russia focusing more on security, and China trying to use the organization to get access to Central Asian oil and gas, both of the bloc's superpowers are united in their commitment to traditional notions of sovereignty and authoritarian rule.

One of the attractions of the SCO for Russia, China and the Central Asian republics is the prospect of halting any new democratizing 'colour revolutions', such as the Rose revolution in Georgia, the Orange revolution in Ukraine, and the so-called 'tulip' revolution in Kyrgyzstan. Moscow and Beijing both gave strong political support to the Uzbek president Islam Karimov when he suppressed pro-democracy demonstrations in Andijan in May 2005, while China has organized counter-insurgency training for several Central Asian police forces.

In political and military terms, the SCO is already showing the potential to turn into a potential rival to NATO in Central Asia: at the 2005 summit in the Kazakh capital of Astana, the SCO members signed a declaration which asked the USA to set a deadline for the withdrawal of its forces from Central Asia. At the 2006 meeting of the SCO – which marked the fifth anniversary of its establishment – SCO members signed a series of agreements on energy co-operation – as well as cocking a snoop at the West by publicly embracing the Iranian leader Mahmood Ahmadinejad. In the long term the SCO could become the kernel of an 'alliance of sovereignty' designed to frustrate Western attempts to interfere in the affairs of other countries to protect human rights or spread democracy. The attractions of its philosophy of 'non-interference' to regimes in the Third World are clear.

Beijing was initially suspicious of regional integration in East Asia, because it feared that the USA would use these groupings to encircle China. But once the Chinese realized that the USA prefers to deal with each of its allies in East Asia – Japan, Australia, the Philippines, Korea and Thailand – individually rather than collectively, it spotted an opportunity for China to emerge as a champion for Asian unity. In 1996, Yan Xuetong persuaded the Foreign Ministry to suggest that the 'New Security Concept' be adopted for the Asian Pacific Region. Qian Qichen, who was foreign minister at the time, made a formal approach to the ASEAN Regional Forum, a grouping led by the ten countries of South-East Asia. Since then China has become increasingly keen on deepening its relationships with its neighbours; its leaders even talk about creating an Asian equivalent of the European Union. In 2004 China called for an ASEAN–China Free Trade Area and to help build an East Asian Community complete with a single currency by 2020.

Yan Xuetong thinks that regional integration will put China's rivals in Asia – the USA and Japan – on the back foot. The USA has become increasingly hostile to regional integration, which it correctly views as a mechanism for China to develop bodies which exclude the USA. American hostility also creates a conundrum for Japan as America's closest ally in the region. Yan Xuetong argues: 'To sustain its special relationship with the United States, Japan has adopted a policy undermining the establishment of the East Asian Community. This policy is similar to that adopted by Great Britain with regard to the European Union. Japan's policy against East Asian regionalization may ultimately weaken its political influence in East Asia.' Yan Xuetong argues that Japan, like Britain in the European context, will always be a reluctant partner wasting valuable political capital on trying to slow the process down, rather than leading from the front in a direction from which it would benefit.

China's liberal internationalists are every bit as keen on the 'New Security Concept' as the neo-comms – but for the opposite reasons. When Qin Yaqing, a rising star among liberal internationalists, was invited to make a presentation to the Politburo in early 2004 he used this rare opportunity to make the case for Chinese engagement with multilateral institutions. But where Yan Xuetong is looking for a mechanism to allow China to project power, Qin Yaqing sees East Asian integration as a way of allowing China to ease the power rivalry with its Asian neighbours – in the same way that the European Union allowed Europe's great powers to trade their bellicosity for harmony.

Qin Yaqing compares China's relations with its neighbours to a giant dealing with dwarves. In the book *Gulliver's Travels*, the diminutive Lilliputians tie down the giant Gulliver with hundreds of tiny cords. Qin Yaqing argues that the same thing needs to happen in Asia. But rather than waiting for the diminutive countries of Asia to take the lead, China needs to tie itself down in order to be able to free itself from suspicion that it is intent on becoming a regional bully. Qin Yaqing sees East Asian integration as the best way for China to bind itself in a series of norms and rules that will not just make it seem less threatening; it will make it lose the will to be threatening: 'Once [China] joined regional co-operation and was no longer a hostile power in the eyes of ASEAN, China changed its attitude toward East Asian regionalism.' Although China, Japan and South Korea together account for 90 per cent of East Asia's economic strength, they have allowed the ten South-East Asian dwarves – that together account for the remaining 10 per cent – to set the pace for regional integration. Qin Yaqing argues that the dwarves have successfully tamed China, using the first East Asia summit in 2005 as an illustration. China abandoned its opposition to Indian and Australian participation in the summit even though it feared that the two countries would gang up with Japan to organize an anti-Chinese caucus within the East Asian Community. 'However,' as Qin Yaqing argued, 'if China had opposed ASEAN's decision it would not only have offended ASEAN, but also aroused mistrust and harmed the co-operative momentum of the region. In order to keep the ball rolling, China had to compromise.' Qin Yaqing is overstating the extent to which regional integration has changed China's attitude to its interests, but China's conversion to Asian unity has certainly enhanced its influence in the region, and reassured its neighbours.

The asymmetric superpower

Although Rear Admiral Yang Yi has emerged as a powerful advocate for increasing China's soft power, his real goal is to earn the legitimacy for a serious build-up in his country's hard power. 'China is a great power,' he says. 'We need to build a powerful military commensurate with our international status.' In an article in *Global Times*, Yang Yi complained of a growing gap between China's economic profile and interests and its capacity to defend them. He fears that the speed at which China's economic interests are expanding – with factories, investments in energy and raw materials, and new markets mushrooming around the world – is outstripping his country's military means to defend them. How, Yang Yi asks, is China going to be able to protect its citizens and assets overseas? How can it take part in disaster relief, anti-terrorist activities, humanitarian assistance or UN peacekeeping missions with its decrepit military machine? And, to return to the perpetual question in Chinese foreign policy circles, how will China be able to defend itself from the USA in the event of a war over Taiwan?

While Yang Yi rarely misses an opportunity to argue for increasing Chinese military spending, he does not want Beijing to get into an arms race with the USA. It has become a truism in Chinese circles that the former Soviet Union spent itself into oblivion by being lured into a competition for military primacy. So rather than trying to match the USA's military machine plane for plane and bomb for bomb, the Chinese approach is to go for an 'asymmetrical' strategy of finding and exploiting the enemy's soft spots. 'Asymmetric warfare' has been voguish in Western military circles for a long time. It has traditionally been used to describe how terrorists can take on and defeat standing armies, in the same way that David took on Goliath. However, the Chinese have taken this debate far beyond the techniques of terrorism. Chinese intellectuals and military planners have created a cottage industry of devising strategies for defeating a 'technologically superior opponent' (their preferred euphemism for the USA).

Every year, Chinese military spending goes up by over 10 per cent (American intelligence estimates that the real figure is two to three times higher) to fulfil the country's great power aspirations. However, its military modernization – which has seen it building ships and submarines, buying fourth-generation combat aircraft and aiming 900 ballistic missiles at Taiwan – has not been about trying to copy or match the US military. The goal is, instead, to find cheaper ways of neutralizing the USA's military advantage. Instead of rivalling the USA on its own ground, Beijing wants to play the Americans at a different game that Beijing can win.

For example, on Taiwan, rather than vainly seeking military supremacy of the Taiwan Strait, Beijing has sought to increase the price the USA would have to pay to defend the island in a war. Twenty years ago the USA could have adopted a purely defensive strategy by creating a shield around the island. As a result of China's military modernization, this defensive strategy is now unsustainable. Now the USA would be put in the unenviable position of needing to attack mainland China to defend Taiwan. China's activities in space have followed a similar pattern. Beijing's goal is not to launch a series of 'Star Wars' against the USA. Instead, it has sought to undermine the US military doctrine by developing weapons which could destroy the satellites which provide so much of the USA's military intelligence. Like Odysseus, who overcame the Cyclops by blinding him with a burning stake, Beijing's audacious plan is to blind American troops by taking away their satellite intelligence. Beijing hopes, thereby, to make it impossible for the USA to get involved in a conflict over Taiwan or Japan.

The most interesting aspects of China's attempt to become an 'asymmetric superpower' are outside the realm of conventional military power. The most detailed explanation of this approach came in a book called *Unrestricted Warfare* which shot into the Chinese best-sellers' lists in 2001. This book, written by two People's Liberation Army colonels, attracted attention only among specialists when it was first published in 1999. However, after Osama bin Laden's attack on the World Trade Center, its thesis seemed visionary. It argues that the American obsession with military hardware is the country's greatest weakness, blinding its policy-makers to the wider picture of military strategy, which must include the use of economic, legal and political weapons as well. The book sets out a series of strategies for 'non-military warfare' arguing that 'soldiers do not have the monopoly of war'.

Top of their list is 'economic warfare'. Referring to the Asian financial crisis of 1997, the authors speak with awe about the power of international financiers like George Soros to undermine the economies of the so-called 'Asian Tigers': 'Economic prosperity that once excited the constant admiration of the Western world changed to a depression, like the leaves of a tree that are blown away in a single night by the autumn wind.' If a lone individual like Soros could unleash so much destruction simply for profit, how much damage could a proud nation like China inflict on the USA with its trillion dollars of foreign reserves?

Another possibility is 'super-terrorism'. In a prescient passage, the authors predicted attacks like Osama bin Laden's on the World Trade Center two years before they took place. They correctly foresaw that the response of the USA to the attacks would be more damaging to the country's security than the attacks themselves: 'it often makes an adversary which uses conventional forces and conventional measures as its main combat strength look like a big elephant charging into a china shop. It is at a loss as to what to do, and unable to make use of the power it has.'

The most interesting thesis is the idea that China could use international law as a weapon, or 'Lawfare' for short. The authors argue that citizens of democracies increasingly demand that their countries uphold international rules, particularly ones that govern human rights and the conduct of war. Governments are, therefore, constrained by regional or worldwide organizations, such as the European Union, ASEAN, the International Monetary Fund, the World Bank, the WTO and the United Nations. The authors argue that China should copy the European model of using international law to pin down the USA: 'there are far-sighted big powers which have clearly already begun to borrow the power of supra-national, multinational, and non-state players to redouble and expand their own influence'. They think that China could turn the United Nations and regional organizations into an amplifier of the Chinese world-view – discouraging the USA from using its might in campaigns like the Iraq War.

Table One
The many facets of unrestricted warfare

MILITARY	TRANS-MILITARY	NON-MILITARY
Atomic warfare	Diplomatic warfare	Financial warfare
Conventional warfare	Network warfare	Trade warfare
Bio-chemical warfare	Intelligence warfare	Resources warfare
Ecological warfare	Psychological warfare	Economic aid warfare
Space warfare	Tactical warfare	Regulatory warfare
Electronic warfare	Smuggling warfare	Sanction warfare
Guerrilla warfare	Drug warfare	Media warfare
Terrorist warfare	Virtual warfare (deterrence)	Ideological warfare

Source: Qiao Liang and Wang Xiangsui, *Unrestricted Warfare* (Beijing: PLA Literature and Arts Publishing House, 1999)

Many of these asymmetric strategies are already taking shape. As the liberal internationalist Shi Yinhong argues, 'the US is winning the military game in the Pacific by strengthening their bases in Guam, Okinawa, Hawaii. China doesn't like it, but it isn't playing that game. China is playing a different game based on economic investment, trade, immigration and smile diplomacy. The USA can't stop this. And it is losing China's game. It can't stop China's rise.' What Shi Yinhong means is that China is trying to change the rules of the competition for primacy in East Asia, and working around the USA rather than confronting it head on. It is as if the USA had an unbeatable team at tennis, so rather than trying to take the Americans on at their game, Beijing is trying to persuade East Asia that table tennis – which China can hope to win at – is the most important game. China's charm offensive is pushing back American influence in countries such as South Korea, but because it is couched in the language of multilateralism and peace it has not alarmed China's neighbours.

Where is China heading?

China is like a giant time machine – straddling centuries of thinking about power. Like Europe it has many twenty-first-century qualities. Its leaders preach a doctrine of stability and social harmony. Its military talk more about soft than hard power. Its diplomats call for multilateralism rather than unilateralism. And its strategists rely more on trade than war to forge alliances and conquer new parts of the world. But China is equally at home in the twentieth-century world of power that the USA has made its own; investing in military modernization, protecting its sovereignty, and talking with a nationalistic fervour about reunification with Taiwan.

It is this twentieth-century China that has undermined claims of peaceful intent and forced the most populous nation in the world into the incongruous position of fearing enemies that include a tiny island with a population of 20 million, the world's most peaceful man (the so-called 'Dalai Lama threat') and a sect that is mainly known for practising t'ai chi and eating vegetables (Falun Gong). The obsessive quest to oppose Taiwanese independence is given as a rationale for double-digit spending increases in defence and the deployment of 700 missiles. It was in part the concern that Taiwan could be goaded into declaring independence by China's perceived softness that led to the dropping of the rhetoric about 'Peaceful Rise'. And Taiwan is just one of the 'five poisons' that the Chinese fear will lead to the break-up of their nation – the others are separatists in the Muslim enclave of Xinjiang, Tibet, Mongolia and the provinces around Korea. Many of the issues that currently cause tension between China and the West – the competition for energy sources, China's role in Africa, stopping nuclear proliferation in Iran and North Korea – can be soothed with tactical shifts by both parties. But for all the talk of multilateralism, soft power and interdependence, the obsession with Taiwan has stopped China from truly adapting its outlook to an era of globalization. Whenever I hear Chinese strategists discussing the small island, I am reminded of the words of Michael Corleone in *The Godfather*: 'Just when I thought I was out, they pull me back in again.'

For a nation that has virtually trademarked a concern for the *longue-durée*, Chinese intellectuals are surprisingly coy about their future. When you ask them what a Chinese hyper-power will be like, they tend to duck the question, trotting out a list of pressing domestic problems which they claim will be all consuming. However, in their more candid moments, China's foreign policy thinkers map out two possible paths.

Liberal internationalists like Zheng Bijian or Qin Yaqing like to talk about how China has rejoined the world; how it is gradually adapting to global norms and learning to make a positive contribution to global order. 'Do you know how many times

Mao went abroad when he was president?' one of my liberal internationalist friends asked me on a recent trip to Beijing. 'Just twice, to Moscow in 1950, and then again in 1957. And do you know how many foreign trips Hu Jintao has made this year alone?' The question was rhetorical because even my friend had lost track of Hu Jintao's dizzying travel schedule. That week alone had seen the shiny-quiffed president hold meetings with leaders from over ten countries, including Algeria, Brazil, Canada, France, India, Japan, Malaysia, Switzerland and the USA. From Darfur to Tehran, Caracas to Havana, Pyongyang to Delhi, Harare to Luanda, China's voice is being heard. The country's voracious appetite for energy, natural resources and markets has propelled its president to the four corners of the earth, forcing this unlikely jet-setter to amass almost as many air-miles as foreign reserves.

And as China becomes more exposed to the world, they argue, so too it is becoming more engaged in solving global problems. In recent years, Beijing has been working through the six-party talks to solve the North Korean nuclear problem; working with the European Union, Russia and the USA on Iran; adopting a conciliatory position on climate change at the Vancouver conference; and sending 4,000 peacekeepers to take part in UN missions. Even on issues where China is at odds with the West – such as on humanitarian intervention – the Chinese position is becoming more nuanced. When the West wanted to intervene in Kosovo, China opposed it on the grounds that it contravened the 'principle of non-intervention'. On Iraq, it abstained. And on Darfur, after blocking measures at the United Nations for many months, China actually voted for a UN mandate for peacekeepers when it was chairing the Security Council. Many Chinese say that Beijing is gradually shifting its position on sovereignty to edge towards humanitarian intervention.

On the other hand, neo-comms like Yan Xuetong openly admit that they are using modern thinking to help China realize ancient dreams. His long-term goal is to see China return to great power status, building an order in its own image. Like many Chinese scholars he has been compulsively studying ancient thought: 'recently I read all these books by ancient Chinese scholars and discovered that these guys are really smart – their ideas are much more relevant than modern International Relations theory'.

The thing that interested him the most was the distinction that ancient Chinese scholars made between two kinds of order: the 'Wang' and the 'Ba'. The 'Wang' system was centred around a dominant superpower, but its primacy was based on benign government rather than coercion or territorial expansion. The 'Ba' system, on the other hand, was a classic 'hegemonic' system, where the most powerful nation imposed order on its periphery through force. Yan explains how in ancient times the Chinese operated both systems: 'Within Chinese Asia we had a "Wang" system. Outside, when dealing with "barbarians", we had a hegemonic system. That is just like the USA today, which adopts a "Wang" system in its relationship with the Western club where it doesn't use military force or employ double standards. On a global scale, however, the USA is hegemonic using military power and employing double standards.'

Yan Xuetong's goal is to recreate an Asian 'Wang' system based on fairness and the rule of law in Asia. The problem for China is getting from here to there without provoking a war with Japan or India. Yan Xuetong's answer goes to the heart of the problem. 'The reason that other countries will accept it is that we would build it through domestic policy by becoming a model society that people would want to be part of. We don't have that yet. At the moment all of China's attractiveness comes from its economic power, but that cannot last. Money worship is not attractive enough. You need moral power.' The unspoken assumption is that China will need to change its political system to be able to become a hyper-power. Yan Xuetong seems to accept that it will be hard for China to have global legitimacy without liberalizing its political system. But surely, even then, Japan would not accept a Chinese-led 'Wang' system? Yan Xuetong's belief in the mechanics of power is absolute: 'Japan will not invite this relationship but over time the Chinese club will be so powerful that Japan will want to join it. It will be like the UK and the EU: a reluctant partner.' According to Yan Xuetong, China will have two options as it becomes more powerful. 'It could become part of the Western "Wang" system. But this will mean changing its political system. The West is talking about this but I do not think they really believe it is possible. The other option is for China to build its own system.'

The tension between the liberal internationalists and the neo-comms is a modern variant of the Mao-era split between bourgeois and revolutionary foreign policy. For the next few years, China will be decidedly bourgeois. It has decided – with some ambivalence – to join the global economy and its institutions. Its goal is to strengthen them in order to pin down the USA and secure a peaceful environment for China's development. But in the long term some Chinese hope to build a global order in China's image. Their approach is to avoid confrontation, while changing the facts on the ground. Just as they are doing in domestic policy, they hope to build pockets of an alternative reality where it is Chinese values and norms that determine the course of events rather than Western ones. Seen from this perspective, the Shanghai Co-operation Organization and East Asia Community are like 'painted zebras' in reverse. Superficially they look like Western models of multilateral integration – like the European Union. But, in reality, they could be seen as the kernels of a Chinese world order where state sovereignty is meaningful and the rights of states to operate without external intervention trump the rights of the citizens that inhabit them.

CONCLUSION

China's Walled World

> There has been much discussion recently about how to 'manage the rise of China. '. . . It gives us a sense of control and mastery, and of paternalistic superiority. With proper piloting and steady nerves on our part, the massive Chinese ship can be brought safely into harbor and put at anchor ... But isn't it possible that China does not want to be integrated into a political and security system that it had no part in shaping? ... Might not China, like all rising powers of the past, including the United States, want to reshape the international system to suit its own purposes, commensurate with its new power?
>
> Robert Kagan, *Washington Post*, Sunday, 15 May 2005

The Western world is abuzz with talk of managing China's rise. How can China be 'moulded', 'socialized' or 'coerced' into becoming like us? How can we make it safe for a world of multilateral institutions, democracy and the rule of law? These questions which diplomats and statesmen compulsively debate are designed to reassure; to make us all believe that China's development is ours to shape. By framing the problem in this way, we can talk ourselves into thinking that with skill and consideration, a new China can be built in our own image. But few Westerners realize that their anguish about China's rise has its mirror image in Beijing. A

115

debate is stirring among Chinese scholars and officials about how to manage the West's decline; how, they are asking, can they best shape the behaviour of Western powers to advance Chinese interests and values?

This controversy burst into the open in 2006 with a provocative newspaper article by Wang Yiwei, a young scholar at Fudan University, who asked 'How can we prevent the USA from declining too quickly?' Wang Yiwei's question generated heated responses from neo-comms and liberal internationalists alike. One of Wang Yiwei's colleagues at Fudan University, Shen Dingli, has framed the challenge even more sharply: 'have people asked themselves what would happen to the world if America declined?' he asked. 'Could China, Russia, the EU, Germany or Japan deliver public goods as America can, or build international political or economic institutions?' For Shen Dingli, who believes that Beijing is not yet ready for prime-time, the goal should be to 'shape an America that is more constrained and more willing to co-operate with the world'. China should use a mix of engagement and containment to shape the USA so that it becomes a responsible power: which, of course, is the exact mirror image of the US approach to China.

What these debates show is that China's rise will not be a mechanical process that can be delicately 'managed' by Western policy-makers. China will actively try to 'manage' the West even as it attempts to manipulate Chinese behaviour. Moreover, the dam-burst of economic growth that has projected the People's Republic into the world is happening at a pace that defies careful 'management', bringing a tsunami of unintended consequences in its wake. In 2005, my friends in Beijing were thrilled to see *The Economist* run a cover story called 'How China Runs the World Economy'. It argued that 'over the coming years, developed countries' inflation and interest rates, wages, profits, oil and even house prices could increasingly be "made in China"'. But two years on, China's economic impact is old news. Soon, the covers of Western magazines will declare that 'China Runs the World's Politics'. I can already imagine editorials arguing that from climate change and nuclear proliferation to human rights and global poverty, the world's policies are being set in Beijing. 'China's ideas on world order,' they will say, 'will have as dramatic an effect on our foreign policies as its cheap exports have had on our economic ones.'

The world according to China

The most immediate consequence of China's rise is that the much predicted 'universalization of Western liberal democracy' has stalled. The Chinese state, with one in five of the world's population, has got off the conveyor belt that seemed to be leading it towards a Western political and economic settlement. Even if the rest of the world carried on developing regardless, this change on its own would overturn Francis Fukuyama's predictions of 'the end of history'.

The next phase of China's development could be even more dramatic. The first thirty years of the People's Republic reform programme have been mainly about China joining the world; absorbing and assimilating know-how from the West on economics, politics and foreign policy. The story of the next thirty years will be about how a more self-confident China reaches out and shapes the world. For governments in Africa, Central Asia, Latin America, and even the Middle East, China's rise means that there is no longer a binary choice between assimilation to the West and isolation. Of course, China will not define the new order on its own, but it will provide an alternative pole and a philosophy that will find their place alongside US attempts to create a balance of power that favours democracy, the European penchant for multi-lateralism and Islamists' hopes of theocratic rule.

The golden thread that links China's emerging ideas about globalization is a quest for control. Chinese thinkers want to create a world where national governments can be masters of their own destiny rather than subject to the whims of global capital and American foreign policy. They want investment, technology and market access from the rest of the world, but they do not want to absorb Western values. Their goal is not to cut China off but rather to allow China to engage with the world on its own terms. In short, they want to stop China being 'flattened' by globalization. Yellow River Capitalism, deliberative dictatorship and Comprehensive National Power are the basic building blocks of this new Chinese philosophy of globalization which seeks to re-establish a place for nation states in controlling the economy, managing politics and shaping the foreign policy agenda. Chinese leaders are already using these ideas – brick by brick – to build an alternative world order: China's 'Walled World'.

The tributaries of the Yellow River

In the spring of 2007, Hu Jintao proudly announced the creation of a new 'Special Economic Zone'. At a packed press conference, business journalists and corporate leaders beamed as he announced that the winning combination of export subsidies, tax-breaks and investments in roads, railways and shipping would be extended to a whole new industrial zone. However, this was a Special Economic Zone with a difference. It was neither on the east coasts of China nor on the western plains. This outpost of Chinese capitalism would be built in the heart of Africa, in the copper-mining belt of Zambia. Standing alongside President Hu

Jintao, the Zambian leader Levy Mwanawasa announced that 'the establishment of a "Special Economic Zone" in Chambishi will see China injecting $800 million into our economy. This will go a long way in boosting economic development in our country.' The Zambian Special Economic Zone is just the first of five that Beijing has pledged to build in Africa as it exports the secrets of Yellow River Capitalism far beyond its borders.

China will literally transplant its growth model into the African continent by building a series of industrial hubs with tax incentives that will be linked by rail, road and shipping lanes to the rest of the world. Zambia will be home to China's 'metals hub', providing the People's Republic with copper, cobalt, diamonds, tin and uranium. The second zone will be in Mauritius, providing China with a 'trading hub' that will give forty Chinese businesses preferential access to the twenty-member state Common Market of East and South Africa that stretches from Libya to Zimbabwe, as well as easy access to the Indian Ocean and South Asian markets. The third zone – a 'shipping hub' – will probably be in the Tanzanian capital, Dar es Salaam. Nigeria, Liberia and the Cape Verde Islands are busy competing for the other two slots.

As it creates these zones, Beijing is embarking on a building spree, criss-crossing the African continent with new roads and railways. The 'Tanzam' railway which China built to link Zambia with Tanzania in the 1970s is being revamped, as is the Benguela line which links Zambia with oil-rich Angola. As one South African puts it, 'even Africa's numerous former colonial powers did not have the commitment to invest so substantially in the continent's infrastructure and probably were unable to afford it anyway'. Many of Africa's former colonial powers have been taken aback by the scale of China's interest in Africa. In November 2006, forty-eight leaders of African nations turned up in Beijing for an elaborate summit hosted by Hu Jintao. At the summit, the Chinese

119

president self-consciously tried to outbid the West by announcing that Chinese aid to Africa would be doubled by 2009 (a full year earlier than the targets which Bob Geldof and Bono demanded of Western governments during the G8); creating a $5 billion investment fund for Africa; a further $5 billion of preferential land and investment credits; debt cancellation for thirty-two countries; thousands of scholarships, as well as a plan to build schools and hospitals across the continent.

More significant than its appeal to African hearts and minds, is the way that China's presence is changing the rules of economic development. The International Monetary Fund and the World Bank used to drive the fear of God into government officials and elected leaders. The development expert Jeffrey Sachs famously compared the IMF to a surrogate government whose seconded officials sat in the inner sanctums of seventy-five developing countries: 'These governments rarely move without consulting the IMF staff, and when they do, they risk their lifelines to capital markets, foreign aid, and international respectability. But today, IMF officials struggle to be listened to even by the poorest countries of Africa. The IMF spent years negotiating a transparency agreement with the Angolan government only to be told hours before the deal was due to be signed that the authorities in Luanda were no longer interested in the money: they had secured a $2 billion soft loan from China. This tale has been repeated across the continent – from Algeria to Chad, Ethiopia to Nigeria, Sudan to Uganda, and Zambia to Zimbabwe.

As the balance of economic power in the world shifts – with Chinese assets of $1.3 trillion dwarfing the IMF's shrinking loans portfolio of $35 billion – the world's most powerful development agencies are struggling to enforce their priorities in the face of Chinese competition. In place of the strict 'conditionality' of the so-called Washington Consensus, many African countries are embracing the lessons of Yellow River Capitalism. Whereas the Washington Consensus is against state intervention in the economy and in favour of privatization, strong property rights and economic 'shock therapy', Yellow River Capitalism encourages the use of public money to drive innovation, a push to protect public property, and the gradualist reforms of Special Economic Zones.

The allure of the Chinese model extends beyond Africa. In their quest to mimic Chinese success, countries as diverse as Brazil, Russia and Vietnam are copying Beijing's activist industrial policy that uses public money and foreign investment to build capital-intensive industries. These countries have also rowed back from another principle of the Washington Consensus and slowed down – sometimes even reversed – the privatization programmes they embarked upon in the 1990s. Just like China, they are maintaining control over sectors of the economy said to be vital to the national interest (and their definitions of the national interest are widening to include public utilities, energy and even agricultural production). Like China, they believe that efficiently managed State Owned Enterprises can raise massive profits for the government, which can be reinvested to achieve political and social goals (and by hanging on to these State Owned Enterprises, the governments can also prevent politically independent entrepreneurs from challenging their powerbase). There are complex reasons for the backlash against the Washington Consensus – the legacy of financial turbulence in Russia, Latin America and Asia, the economic freedom accorded to resource-rich nations by the rise in commodities prices, and the election of populist leaders in many parts of the world – but the stunning success of China's economy is clearly part of the picture.

What is striking is that the spread of Yellow River Capitalism seems to be going far beyond the regions that have been targeted by Chinese investors. The success of China's model of gradualist change has led to the creation of a rash of Special Economic Zones all over the world. According to World Bank estimates, by 2007 there were more than 3,000 projects taking place in Special Economic Zones in 120 countries worldwide. Most are explicitly modelled on the Chinese example. The Chinese model has attracted admirers across the developing world. Government research teams from Iran to Egypt, Angola to Zambia, Kazakhstan to Russia, India to Vietnam and Brazil to Venezuela have been crawling around the Chinese cities and countryside in search of lessons from Beijing's experience.

Just as attractive as Chinese growth is the way that Beijing has been able to maintain control over its own economic policies. Unlike the Asian Tigers of the 1980s which relied on economic assistance from the West, China has freed itself from the interference of Western development agencies and financial institutions. China has happily resisted vocal pressure from the USA to revalue its currency, making it clear that it would deal with this issue on its own terms. For developing countries that exchanged colonial rule for the diktats of the IMF and World Bank, the promise of setting their own agenda is the stuff that dreams are made of. As one Nigerian journalist puts it:

> The Chinese government knows what is good for its people and therefore shapes its economic strategy accordingly. Its strategy is not informed by the Washington Consensus. China had not allowed any [IMF] or World Bank official to impose on it some neo-liberal package of reforms . . . their strategy has not been a neo-liberal overdose of deregulation, cutting social expenditure, privatizing everything under the sun and jettisoning the public good. They have not branded subsidy a dirty word.

For many years, developing countries were uncomfortable with the 'flat world' philosophy of the Washington Consensus. However, it was not until recently that they had a proven alternative of combining gradualist economic reforms with the state control and social priorities of Yellow River Capitalism. Globalization was supposed to bring about the worldwide triumph of the market economy, but China is showing that state capitalism is one of its biggest beneficiaries.

Deliberative dictatorship

As free market ideas have spread across the world, liberal democracy has often travelled in its wake. In the last thirty years alone more than sixty countries have embraced democracy. The American scholar Samuel Huntington has christened this the 'Third Wave of Democratization' (the first wave was in the early 1800s, the second took place immediately after the Second World War). Even in the last three years, we have seen popular protests demanding democracy on the streets of Georgia, Ukraine, Lebanon and Kyrgyzstan – the so-called 'colour revolutions'.

But for the authorities in Beijing there is nothing inexorable about the progress of liberal democracy. I was in China at the time of Ukraine's 'Orange' revolution and Kyrgyzstan's so-called 'tulip' revolution. My Chinese hosts looked on in disbelief as Moscow failed to stem the popular protests and shore up its preferred candidates. In their determination not to repeat what they regarded as Russian mistakes, the Chinese authorities set up a unit to review the work of foreign NGOs in China, while one of the leading government-sponsored think-tanks sent researchers to Uzbekistan, Kyrgyzstan, Ukraine, Georgia and Belarus to assess the role of pro-democracy NGOs and to propose countermeasures. The

Chinese government decided that they did not want any 'colour revolutions' happening on their watch, and have therefore cracked down on foreign-funded NGOs and sent teams of people to train other governments in Central Asia on effective crowd dispersal.

Today, the talk among Western democracy activists is of a backlash against democracy promotion. The American NGO Freedom House has coined the term 'freedom stagnation' to explain the fact that the number of free countries in the world has not increased. The National Endowment for Democracy talks about 'a "chilling effect" on democracy assistance, intimidating some groups and activists, and making it more difficult for them to receive and utilize international assistance and solidarity'. Leading writers about democracy, such as Tom Carothers, describe a 'pushback' against democracy, as autocratic governments clamp down on free media, civil society and human rights groups.

Of course, this is not all down to China. The Bush administration's 'forward agenda for freedom' which linked democracy promotion to regime change in Iraq has sapped the legitimacy of democracy promotion, and provided a pretext for governments to crack down on human rights and democracy activists. President Putin in Russia has led a crackdown on the media and political freedom in his own country and supported regimes in the former Soviet Union that have adopted the same tactics. And many recent democratic set-backs such as the military coups in Thailand and Congo-Brazzaville had little to do with China. However, China must take some responsibility for this trend.

Even if the People's Republic had done nothing in the world, the power of the Chinese example would have presented a major challenge to promoters of democracy. The contrast between its performance and that of the Soviet Union has given rise to a widespread belief that economic reform must precede political reform.

This 'sequencing myth' has become a major barrier for promoters of democracy, taking the pressure off many countries to liberalize their political systems. Even more worrying, China's economic success has broken the perceived link between democracy and growth. Even aid agencies in democratic countries, such as the UK's Department for International Development, freely admit that there is no evidence that democracy contributes to economic development. And if China's recent experiments with deliberative dictatorship and public consultation work, dictatorships around the world will take heart from a model that allows one-party states to survive in an era of globalization and mass communications.

Many people argue over whether China is actively promoting autocracy around the world, or whether it simply has a morally neutral approach that puts its national interest first. Either way, through its political and economic links with problematic regimes, China has emerged as the biggest champion of autocracy around the world. The pressure group Human Rights Watch complains that 'China's growing foreign aid program creates new options for dictators who were previously dependent on those who insisted on human rights progress'. China's support goes beyond its increasingly generous economic aid. It offers friendly regimes political support at the United Nations Security Council, training in counter-insurgency, and even access to bugging and surveillance equipment.

In Zimbabwe, the Chinese government has given President Mugabe political, military and technical support. The Chinese have frustrated attempts in the United Nations to explore his 'Operation Clean the Filth' that resulted in the mass eviction of 700,000 urban poor. Beijing has also provided Mugabe with technology for autocracy, supplying him with equipment to jam radio signals, monitor e-mails and disperse demonstrations. After Uzbekistan's government massacred hundreds of protesters at

Andijan in 2005, the country's president Islam Karimov was rewarded with red carpet treatment in Beijing, a $600 million oil deal, and offers of police training for crowd dispersal.

China is the largest investor in Burma and the authorities have propped up an increasingly oppressive regime with economic aid, investment and military technology. China provides low-interest loans to the Burmese government, most recently a June 2006 pledge of $200 million to five unspecified government ministries. China also supplies 90 per cent of Burma's armaments and has granted $1.6 billion in military assistance and modernization funding. China has dispatched teams of advisers to persuade the Burmese authorities to implement political reform as a means of relieving international pressure. According to one source, 'this is likely to involve borrowing some significant components from the Chinese system – and may mean adopting a National People's Congress approach to parliamentary democracy'. Chinese actions have not simply prevented the regime from collapsing, they have also caused India to overturn its previous policy of isolation (Delhi was worried about Rangoon falling into the Chinese sphere of influence).

China will not go to the wall to support failing regimes. Following pressure from the West, it has shifted its tactics on Sudan, Zimbabwe and Burma. But these tactical shifts do not change the fact that China will never be supportive of multi-party elections and human rights: why would it promote rights for foreigners that it denies to its own citizens?

Comprehensive National Power

'It must be difficult and occasionally irritating to find yourselves the recipient of every demand, to be called upon in every crisis, to be expected always and everywhere to do what needs to be done.' That is how the former British prime minister Tony Blair addressed the American people in 1999, when genocide was raging through Kosovo. He was delivering his call to action in the only nation that could stop the killing. 'Acts of genocide can never be a purely internal matter,' he declared, outlining his 'new doctrine of international community' that authorized powerful states to protect the citizens of other countries from massive abuses of human rights. But, with the USA bogged down in Iraq and Afghanistan, today's campaigners on global issues are focusing more and more of their attention on Beijing. It is not entirely surprising that China has been called upon to deal with problems in neighbouring countries such as North Korea or Burma, but who would have thought that China would be in the front line of global discussions on climate change, nuclear proliferation in Iran or land reform in Zimbabwe? The most dramatic development is possibly the fact that Beijing is in the eye of the gathering storm in Darfur.

In July 2007, the American speed-skater and Olympic gold medallist Joey Cheek led a delegation to the Chinese embassy in Washington DC. He argued that Beijing's relationship with Khartoum 'gives China the opportunity to do something that no one else in the world is able to do. It gives them a chance to show that they truly are the power in the world that they are aspiring to be, and that they could pull off something that the West couldn't.' Beijing is under pressure to use its leverage on the Sudanese government: as well as selling the government weapons, it buys two-thirds of Sudan's oil and has invested $6 billion in its industry. More importantly, it is China that has set the pace for international diplomacy both in Darfur itself and in the United Nations in New York, watering down various attempts to introduce sanctions and mandate UN peacekeepers (the United Nations Security Council has only banned travel and frozen the

127

assets of four junior individuals in a conflict that has seen the death of 400,000 people and the displacement of 2 million).

China has been treading a fine line on Darfur. Smarting from accusations of 'bank-rolling genocide', it has tried not to appear destructive: appointing an envoy to Darfur in 2007, supporting the idea of a UN peacekeeping mission, pressurizing the Sudanese government to negotiate with rebel forces. But, at the same time, Beijing has stuck to a line of 'influence, not intervention', refusing to accept sanctions against the regime, and insisting that forces should only be deployed with the Sudanese government's consent. In its approach to the crisis, Beijing has sought to use multilateralism to increase its own power and that of its Sudanese ally – sticking to the idea that everything needs to be passed through the United Nations Security Council (where China has a veto), and promoting the idea of multilateral talks. This echoes the Chinese approach to North Korea and Burma where Beijing has promoted talks which allow it to set the pace of diplomacy, delivering just enough progress to satisfy the West but not so much as to endanger the autocratic regimes which look to China for support.

China's approach to Darfur shows that its emerging 'Walled World' philosophy has revolutionary implications for geopolitics. At the beginning of the twenty-first century, Western governments and their citizens, influenced by genocide in Rwanda, terrorist camps in Afghanistan and nuclear proliferation in Iran, began to feel a responsibility to intervene in countries that threaten human rights and international security. However, Beijing is determined to defend an older idea of sovereignty, based around the sovereign rights of states. Its rules include not invading other countries, not trying to overthrow regimes, and above all not interfering in the internal affairs of other states. In the place of Tony Blair's 'international community' they are pushing 'Comprehensive National Power'.

China is promoting this agenda internationally through its new-found interest in multilateralism. By supporting the United Nations and creating new regional organizations, Beijing is not only changing the balance of power in many parts of the world, but also ensuring the importance of respect for national sovereignty. The Western creations of the European Union and NATO – defined by an approach that includes the pooling rather than the protecting of sovereignty – have found their matches in the Chinese-inspired East Asian Community and Shanghai Co-operation Organization. Through these organizations, China is reassuring its neighbours of its peaceful intent and creating a new community of interest that excludes the USA. The former US official Susan Shirk draws a parallel between China's multilateral diplomacy and her own country's after the Second World War: 'the United States was . . . able to convince other countries that it would not threaten them by creating multilateral global institutions and submitting itself to the authority of these institutions. By binding itself to international rules and regimes, the United States successfully established a hegemonic order. Could China's participation in global and regional multilateral institutions have the same result, enabling China to rise to power without provoking a concerted effort to contain it?'

The United Nations is becoming a powerful amplifier of the Chinese world-view. Unlike Russia which comports itself with a swagger – enjoying its ability to overtly frustrate US and EU plans – China tends to opt for a conciliatory posture. It is prepared to veto things when it has to, but it prefers to hide behind others, and block things without getting the blame. In the run-up to the Iraq War, although China opposed military action it allowed France, Germany and Russia to lead the international opposition to it. In 2005 when there was a debate about enlarging the United Nations Security Council, China encouraged African countries to demand their own seat with a veto which effectively killed off Japan's bid for a permanent Security Council seat. Equally, Beijing has been willing to allow the Organization of Islamic States to take the lead in weakening the new Human Rights Council. This subtle diplomacy has been devastatingly effective – contributing to a massive fall in US influence: in 1995 the USA won 50.6 per cent of the votes in the United Nations general assembly; by 2006, the figure had fallen to just 23.6 per cent. On human rights, the results are even more dramatic: China's win-rate has rocketed from 43 per cent to 82 per cent, while the USA's has tumbled from 57 per cent to 22 per cent. The *New York Times'* UN correspondent James Traub has detected a paradigm shift in the United Nations' operations: 'it's a truism that the Security Council can function only insofar as the United States lets it. The adage may soon be applied to China as well.' James Traub may be right. China's capacity to influence the United Nations is increasing, and soon we may be complaining about Chinese behaviour on big policy issues, rather than saying 'if only the USA would act differently'.

The China Model

In the 1990s, the satirical writer Wang Shuo upset the Chinese authorities by penning a best-selling novel, *Please Don't Call Me Human*, in which he imagined a Beijing Olympics where nations competed to prove their citizens' capacity for humiliation, rather than their athletic prowess. In this fantasy competition – which China was determined to win at any cost – the novel's protagonist, a delinquent pedicab driver called Yuanbao, who leads the Chinese team, scored the maximum points by performing a number of degrading rituals ranging from drinking another contestant's urine to being frozen alive in a fish tank. Wang Shuo's remorseless mocking of his country's greatest obsession – saving face – ends with the distressing scene of Yuanbao ripping off his own face to win the gold medal. The image of the faceless anti-hero standing in a pool of blood – holding his facial skin above his head in triumph – was such a shocking rebuke to the country's dreams of national greatness that Wang Shuo's writings were eventually banned in a government campaign against 'spiritual pollution'. The country that Wang Shuo depicts had become so used to seeing the world order as a given to which it must adapt that it assumed that the only way to overturn the humiliation inflicted on China by foreigners was to embrace that humiliation itself.

On the surface, the Beijing that is preparing to host the real Olympics in 2008 could not be more different from that depicted in Wang Shuo's novel. At home, the regime sees the games as China's coming-out party as a global superpower. The generation that lived with the weight of national humiliation is giving way to a new elite whose working lives have only known Chinese success and prestige. And abroad, China hype has become ubiquitous: almost half the leaders of the world's 192 countries visited China in 2006 to pay tribute to the rising giant. However, for all this show of confidence, China's mindset remains defensive. Like Wang Shuo's Olympic Committee, China's contemporary philosophers are trying to change the rules of global competition to reflect China's strengths, rather than having the confidence to compete with the West on existing terms. This defensiveness has a history.

Almost all visitors to Beijing make the pilgrimage to the Temple of Heaven, whose lantern-like profile rises like a spectre over the Chinese capital, offering its citizens an iconic glimpse of the afterlife. The intricately structured building – whose form was designed according to cosmological principles to mimic the exact shape of heaven – rises through a series of white marble clouds before reaching a plateau at the 'Altar of Heaven'. It was here that the emperor – the so-called 'Son of Heaven' – would offer sacrifices and prayers to 'the Supreme Ruler of the Universe'. His annual re-enactment of this ritual was designed to symbolize the principle of world order in ancient China, the concept of 'all-under-heaven' or 'Tian-xia'. The emperor was literally at the centre of the world order, and his rule would recognize no boundaries or limits. But even as they were flaunting their universalist ambitions at their favourite temple, the Ming emperors were building an even more famous national symbol: the Great Wall of China. The very act of opening up and looking at the world, seemed to carry with it a need to establish boundaries which could shield China from the influence of barbarians and foreigners. The Ming dynasty, like every regime in Chinese history, was obsessed with the need to hold China together and shield it from its neighbours. The Chinese have labelled this obsession with boundaries the 'Great Wall mentality'. It is a concern that runs so deep that it has infiltrated the country's identity, its lifestyle and even its alphabet: all Chinese cities are surrounded by walls, the traditional Chinese courtyard house literally takes the form of a wall surrounding an atrium, while the pictograph for 'country' is made up of a four-walled pattern.

Although China's concern with national sovereignty and the power of the state arose at a time when China feared incursions from foreign powers, these ideas are now being projected on to the world outside. Today's 'Great Wall mentality' is not about protecting the country from foreign incursions; it is about promoting a Chinese view of sovereignty. This is not happening according to a pre-calculated master plan. China is so big, so pragmatic and so desperate to succeed that its political leadership is constantly experimenting with new ways of doing things. It used its Special Economic Zones to test out a different kind of market philosophy.

Now it is testing a thousand other ideas – from public consultations to regional alliances. But from this laboratory of social experiments, a new world-view is emerging that will in time crystallize into a recognizable Chinese model. And China's own emancipation from the West has created an alternative, non-Western path for the rest of the world to follow. The ideal of a 'Walled World' where nation states can trade with each other on global markets but maintain their control over their economic future, their political system and their foreign policy is emerging as an ideological challenge both to the US philosophy of a 'flat world' and the European preference for liberal multilateralism. In this new competitive environment Western policy-makers will need to adapt their own ideas if they want to promote and protect their liberal values.

The twenty-first century will not be a Chinese century where McDonald's is replaced by *mantou* (steamed buns) as the world's favourite fast food, CNN is subordinated by CCTV, or Hollywood by the Chinese New Wave. But China will join the USA and the European Union as a shaper of world order, challenging Western influence in Africa, Asia, the Middle East, Latin America and the former Soviet Union with a different model of globalization. If China continues to grow, it is possible to imagine that in the future, demonstrators outside the World Trade Organization will complain about the Beijing Consensus as well as the Washington Consensus. They may tune into the Chinese president's address to the National People's Congress as well as the American 'State of the Union'. The political struggle between Xi and Li could be as overreported as the contests between Ségolène Royal and Nicolas Sarkozy, or Rudi Giuliani and Hillary Clinton. The world's media may become as obsessed with China's neo-comms' plans for Central Asia, as they were with the American Neo-Cons' designs for the Middle East. And when Bono and Bob Geldof next attempt to save Africa, they may hold their largest concert in Beijing's Olympic Stadium rather than London's Hyde Park.

China's path to superpower status will not be smooth. It is possible that Beijing's formula of state capitalism, open markets and a closed political system will not last the course. However, it is worth noting that it took three generations for a Soviet economic model that did not work in theory to actually fail in practice. And until the very moment that it collapsed, the Soviet Union embodied an alternative model that challenged Western liberal democracy. Beijing's ascent has already changed the balance of economic and military power, and it is now changing the world's ideas about politics, economics and order. Those who argued that the People's Republic would become more Western with its growing wealth have been proven wrong. For the first time since the end of the Cold War, Europe and America face a formidable alternative: the Chinese model.

DRAMATIS PERSONAE

Cui Zhiyuan is a professor of Politics and Public Management at the Tsinghua University in Beijing. A leading member of the 'New Left', he became well known in Chinese intellectual circles through his work on alternatives to neo-liberal capitalism. His most famous works were a book on Nanjie village and an article calling for a 'Second Liberation of Thought'. He was born in 1963, when his father was in Sichuan as a nuclear engineer. Cui studied at Hunan University, then started a masters at the Chinese Academy of Social Sciences (CASS) in Beijing, which he did not finish, before going to Chicago University in 1987. He moved back to China in 2004 because his parents were old and he is an only child. 'The intellectual debates in the 1990s migrated to where the scholars were – and where they were able to get published, above all Hong Kong. You could be more influential outside China because you couldn't say much here. But today it is much freer and the internet has made a world of difference. As long as you don't write that the Communist Party should be overthrown immediately, you can write what you like.'

Fang Ning is a leading thinker on political theory. His most famous work is the best-selling ultra-nationalist tract that he co-authored with Wang Xiaodong, *China's Road under the Shadow of Globalization* (1999). Fang Ning is especially proud of his 1997 article 'Socialism is about Harmony', which was one of the first to make a connection between socialism and harmony. He claims

135

that his article was one of the inspirations for the now popular political slogans 'Harmonious Society' and 'Harmonious World'. As the Deputy Director of the Institute of Politics at the Chinese Academy of Social Sciences, he is a prolific writer on Chinese political theory and democracy. He has worked closely with the Chinese government on several projects, including the 2005 'White Paper on Democracy'.

Gan Yang is an academic with 'New Left' sympathies. Currently working as a research fellow at the Centre for Asian Studies at the University of Hong Kong, he obtained a PhD at the University of Chicago after travelling to the United States in the wake of the Tiananmen protests. His major works include *We are Creating Tradition* (1989) and *Reflections on Liberalisms* (1997). Gan Yang upset many people on the New Right when he provocatively used the phrase 'creative destruction' to describe the Cultural Revolution.

Hu Angang is the *enfant terrible* of Chinese economics. With his spiky hair and informal style he has rocked the staid Chinese academy with the same zeal that the British Nigel Kennedy did with the world of classical music. The report on 'China's state capacity', which he co-authored with Wang Shaoguang while at Yale, has been widely regarded as one of the most influential works on China's political economy in the past two decades – convincing the government to strengthen the role of the state. He is the author of over forty publications and is a regular consultant for China's central and provincial governments. He is now Professor and Director of the Centre for China Studies at the School of Public Policy and Management at Tsinghua University. He met Wang Shaoguang during a period of post-doctoral study at Yale University and has since been a visiting professor in a number of Western universities. As China's most influential 'New Left' economist, he is a pioneer of research into China's 'national circumstances', an interest he developed initially in the Chinese Academy of Science in 1985.

Pan Wei is a professor in the School of International Studies and Director of the Centre for China and Global Affairs, both at Beijing University, and one of the rising stars in Chinese academia. His paper on 'Consultative Rule of Law', which calls on China to model its political system on Singapore rather than Western liberal democracies, has been very influential. He obtained his PhD from the University of California at Berkeley in 1996. He is one of China's most original thinkers on political reform and political and economic development in rural China. Pan Wei has a 'conservative' orientation, advocating a Chinese model of political and economic development.

Qin Yaqing is Professor and executive vice-president of China's Foreign Affairs University. He has built up a reputation as one of the most dovish experts on foreign policy in China. He obtained his PhD from the University of Missouri in 1994. He combines an important role in a government-sponsored body – the Foreign Affairs University was set up by the veteran Chinese foreign minister Zhou En Lai to play the same role in foreign policy as the Central Party School does in domestic policy – with a passion for international relations theory. A strong advocate for a 'Chinese school of international relations', he has also been involved with the Chinese government's foreign policy making, advising on issues such as East Asian regional integration.

Shi Yinhong is Professor of International Relations at Beijing's People's University. He is one of the most interesting thinkers about China's Grand Strategy, and provoked controversy with his proposals for détente with Japan. He has been a visiting fellow at many American universities such as Harvard University, University of North Carolina and Denver. An expert on grand strategy, Shi Yinhong is something of a 'liberal internationalist' who takes a moderate stance on relations with the United States and Japan.

Wang Hui is Research Professor at Tsinghua University and was co-editor of China's leading intellectual journal *Dushu* from 1996 to 2007. He is one of the leading members of China's 'New Left', a loose grouping of scholars who have been calling for the Chinese government to pay more attention to inequality and environmental pollution. He was born into a family of intellectuals in Jiangsu in 1959. During the Cultural Revolution, after graduating from middle school, he became a worker in a textile factory for twenty months. He then went to Xingdu University before doing a PhD at the Chinese Academy of Social Sciences in 1985. Wang Hui took part in the demonstrations in Tiananmen Square in June 1989. He went to Harvard in 1992, followed by some time at the University of California at Los Angeles. 'When I was at middle school we went to the countryside every spring and autumn to work with peasants so I am familiar with any kind of agricultural production.'

Wang Shaoguang is one of the most creative thinkers in the 'New Left'. A professor at the Chinese University of Hong Kong and editor of *The China Review*, he has lived outside China for most of the last two decades. A former Red Guard, he obtained a PhD from Cornell University on the Cultural Revolution in 1990 and taught at Yale University from 1990–2000 before moving to Hong Kong. The 1993 work he co-authored with Hu Angang,

China's State Capacity Report, stimulated a massive debate within China that eventually led to a major reform of the tax system. Since then the two have written several other influential reports on Chinese political economy which have influenced the government's policy making. More recently he has collaborated with Pan Wei and Gan Yang on a research project on the China Model.

Wang Xiaodong is China's most famous and high-brow 'ultra-nationalist', who is often at the forefront of controversy whether it is in debates about China–US relations, China–Japan relations, or the latest discussion on China's environmental problem. The book *China's Road under the Shadow of Globalization*, which he co-authored with Fang Ning in 1999, is the manifesto for a new wave of Chinese nationalism in an age of globalization. Although he is not in the mainstream of China's foreign policy community, he is widely respected and has built links with a number of 'princelings', the children of high-ranking officials.

Yan Xuetong is China's leading 'neo-comm', an assertive nationalist who has called for a more forthright approach to Taiwan, Japan and the United States. As Director of the Institute of International Studies at Tsinghua University, he is one of the most famous foreign policy thinkers in China. He obtained his PhD from the University of California at Berkeley in 1992. He worked as research fellow at the China Institute of Contemporary International Relations in Beijing during 1982–4 and 1992–2000.

Yang Yao is one of the few economists to study the implications of elections and grass-roots democracy on social welfare. He is Professor and Deputy Director of the China Centre for Economic Research at Beijing University. He obtained his PhD from the University of Wisconsin-Madison in 1996. Yang Yao distances himself both from the market fundamentalism of most of his fellow economists who make up the 'New Right', and the 'populist tendencies' of the 'New Left'. 'Economists in China are much more right-wing than in Europe or America,' he says. 'I am left-wing because I got my PhD from Wisconsin which is one of the most socialist states in the USA. I didn't realize at the time that Wisconsin had so much influence on me.'

Yang Yi joined the Chinese navy in 1968 and was a naval attaché in the Chinese embassy in Washington from 1995–2000. He is now Director of the Institute of Strategic Studies at the PLA's National Defense University. He leads the university's research on China's international strategy and national security strategy. He is a respected officer and scholar, and a leading authority on Chinese security policy. In recent years he has published several influential articles on national security in the *Global Times*, which have attracted attention both within and outside China.

Yu Keping is Deputy Director of the Central Compilation and Translation Bureau. His centre has been at the forefront of moves to analyse and spread the lessons from experiments in grass-roots democracy, elections and public consultations. Spoken of as an informal aide to President Hu Jintao, Yu Keping caused controversy with articles drawn from his 2006 book *Democracy is a Good Thing*. He obtained his PhD in political science from Beijing University in 1988 and is a rising star on Chinese communist political theory. Apart from his many academic positions, he is also the chief expert of a new government-sanctioned task-force on Marxism research, a renewed research area that has increasingly become a focus for many of China's best political theorists. Although he has also held government posts, he is generally well regarded by the academic community for his scholarly research.

Along with Fang Ning and a few others, he is the most watched Chinese theorist on the Chinese style of democracy.

Zheng Bijian has been one of China's most influential and controversial thinkers on foreign policy and political reform. He has a distinguished academic and official career, starting with a teaching position at People's University and working his way up to become the executive vice-minister of China's Propaganda Department and Vice-President of the Central Party School. He is said to be a close adviser to the Chinese president Hu Jintao. In the 1970s and 1980s he emerged as an important champion of reform, drafting major speeches and party documents. Most importantly he wrote Deng Xiaoping's key speeches on his famous 1992 'Southern tour' which recommitted China to economic reform in the wake of Tiananmen. In 2004 he organized a research project which launched the idea of 'peaceful rise'. Although 'peaceful rise' is seen to have failed as both an intellectual endeavour and political project, many of its ideas continue to find resonance in the current Chinese foreign policy community. Currently he is President of China Reform Forum, a semi-official research institution that advises the Chinese government. Most recently he has been engaged in a project on China's cultural rejuvenation.

Zhang Weiying is one of China's most famous economists, and a leading member of the 'New Right'. He is the First Associate Dean of Guanghua School of Management of Beijing University, and Director of the Institute of Business Research of Beijing University and e-Business Center. Named as 'The Man of the Year in Chinese Economy' by Chinese Central Television (CCTV) in 2002, he serves on several governmental and corporate boards. He obtained his PhD from Oxford University under the supervision of the winner of the 1996 Nobel Prize in Economics, James Mirrlees.

Before going to Oxford in 1990, he had been working as a researcher in the theory and policy of economic reform in the now defunct Commission for State Institutional Reform and was the first to put forward the idea of 'dual-track price reform' in China. He is a leading authority on enterprise theory in China, influential in the academic, government and business communities. He is widely regarded as the champion of the neoliberal school in China for his policy prescriptions on China's economic development. As such, he is also one of the most criticized economists in China today.

NOTES

Many of the quotations from Chinese thinkers in the book come from interviews with the author. I have not footnoted these direct quotations in order not to over-burden the reader with notes.

Introduction

p. 5   **China's very existence** Gan Yang, 'The Grand Three Traditions in the New Era: The Integration of the Three Traditions and the Re-emergence of the Chinese Civilization', lecture at Tsinghua University in Beijing, 2006 (translated by Zhang Feng)

p. 10   **Build a dream** Victor Hugo, An Open Letter by Victor Hugo Condemning the burning of Yuanmingyuan by French and British Troops in 1860. English translation available at
http://www.pbase.com/chlorophyl/image/69158121

p. 13   **The American dream is the highest ideal** Yu Keping, 'Americanization, Westernization, Signification, Modernization or Globalization of China?'

p.14   **Reverse racism** Wang Xiadong 'Chinese Nationalism under the Shadow of Globalisation', unpublished lecture at London School of Economics, 7 February 2005

p. 14   **Chinese intellectuals** Cui Zhiyuan, *Second Liberation of Thought* (Hong Kong: Oxford University Press, 1997)

p. 14 **In the 1980s I went** Wang Xiadong, 'Chinese Nationalism Under the Shadow of Globalisation', unpublished lecture at London School of Economics, 7 February 2005

p. 15 **Today we can see** Gan Yang, 'The Grand Three Traditions in the New Era: The Integration of the Three Traditions and the Re-emergence of the Chinese Civilization', lecture at Tsinghua University in Beijing, 2006 (translated by Zhang Feng)

Chapter One

p. 21 **Fifty years before the building was begun** Franz Kafka, *Great Wall of China* (London: Penguin, 2005)

p. 21 **Economics acquired the force of an ethics** Wang Hui, 'The New Criticism', in Wang Chaohua (ed.), *One China, Many Paths* (London: Verso, 2003)

p. 21 **131 of 274 independent directors** Zhang Hongyi, 'Capitalists and Economists in the New China', Evan Jones blog, http//alertandalarmed.blogspot.com

p. 21 **derisively known as *fanshipai* or 'whateverists'** After Mao died, he was succeeded by Hua Guofeng who pronounced what became known as the 'two whatevers policy' (the party should 'support whatever policy decisions Chairman Mao made and follow whatever instructions Chairman Mao gave'). After Deng Xiaoping came to power, conservatives who stubbornly stuck to Maoist policies became known as the 'Whatever Faction'.

p. 23 **Zhang Weiying has a favourite** Edward S. Steinfeld, '"Painted Horses": Reform Culture and the Phenomenon of Partial Reform', MIT, October 2003, to be published in Edward S. Steinfeld, *China's Market Visions*, forthcoming

p. 23 **the theory of 'dual-track pricing'** Fan Gang, *China's 'Dual-Track Transition' Toward the Market: Achievements* *and Problems,* Issue Papers (Burlingame, CA: The 1990 Institute)

p. 26 **As a result** Ibid.

p. 27 **ban on maritime activity** Su Xiaokang and Wang Luxiang, *Deathsong of the river: a reader's guide to the Chinese TV series Heshang,* introduced, translated and annotated by Richard W. Bodman and Pin P. Wan (Ithaca: East Asia Program, Cornell University 1991)

p. 28 **In the early morning** Wang Hui, *China's New Order: Society, Politics, and Economy in Transition* (Cambridge, MA: Harvard University Press, 2003)

p. 29 **social and economic demands** Ibid.

p. 30 **Just as people** Ibid.

p. 31 **those who thought** Ibid.

p. 33 **China is caught** Jehangir S. Pocha, 'China's New Left', *New Perspectives Quarterly,* 22 (2) (2005), 25–31

p. 35 **was immortalized** Cui Zhiyuan, Deng Yingtao and Miao Zhuang, *Nanjie Village* (Beijing: Dangdai Zhongguo Chubanshe, 1996)

p. 36 **The present experience** Cui Zhiyuan and Roberto Mangabeira Unger, 'China in the Russian Mirror', *New Left Review,* I/208, November–December 1994

p. 37 **weakest in the world** Hu Angang and Wang Shaoguang, *Strengthen the leading role of the central government in the transition to a market economy: A research report on China's state capacity* (Shenyang: Liaoning Renmin Chubanshe, 1993)

p. 37 **They showed that** Cited in Joseph Fewsmith, *China since Tiananmen: the politics of transition* (Cambridge: Cambridge University Press, 2001)

p. 37 **as powerful as the central government** In the course of the 1980s the percentage of this 'extra-budgetary revenue' rose from 31 per cent of budgeted revenue in 1978 to 95 per cent in 1989

p. 37 **15 per cent of China's GDP** Hu Angang, 'Corruption: An Enormous Black Hole – Public Exposure of Economic Costs as a Result of Corruption', in Hu Angang, *Great Transformations in China* (Beijing: Centre for Chinese Studies, Tsinghua University, 2005)

p.38 **most powerful argument** Jahanger Aziz and Li Cui, 'Explaining China's Slow Consumption: the neglected role of household income', (Washington: IMF, 2007)

p. 39 **for reasons of efficiency and principle** Zhang Honyi, 'Capitalists and Economists in the New China', Evan Jones blog, http//alertandalarmed.blogspot.com

p. 41 **Already a quarter of China's land** Hu Angang, 'Why Does China's Economy Grow So Fast?', in *Great Transformations in China* (Beijing: Centre for China Studies, Tsinghua University, 2005)

p. 41 **animal and human waste** Elizabeth C. Economy, 'The Great Leap Backward', *Foreign Affairs*, 86 (5) (September/ October 2007)

p. 42 **gross domestic product** China issues first "green GDP" report, Chinadialogue.net (7 September 2006)

p. 43 **China's economic miracle** Andrea Lorenz, 'China's Environmental Suicide: a Government Minister Speaks', English edition of *Der Spiegel*, April 2005

p. 43 **attracted tens of thousands of people** Elizabeth C. Economy, 'The Great Leap Backward', *Foreign Affairs*, 86 (5) (September/October 2007)

p. 43 **Green GDP reporting** 'China silences green GDP study, report says', Reuters, 23 July 2007

p. 44 **compared to just 150,000 today** C. Fred Bergsten, Bates Gill, Nicholas R. Lardy and Derek Mitchell, *China: The Balance*

Sheet: What the World Needs to Know about the Emerging Superpower (New York: PublicAffairs Books, 2007)

p. 44   **or 45 million jobs** Ibid.

p. 44   **Bureaucrats . . . do not bear risks** Zhang Weiying, 'China's SOE Reform: A Corporate Governance Perspective', working paper, Beijing University, 1998

p. 44   **the state owns 60 per cent** Harry G. Gelber, *The Dragon and the Foreign Devils: China and the World, 1100 BC to the Present* (London: Bloomsbury, 2007)

p. 45   **barely a third** Edward S. Steinfeld, '"Painted Horses": Reform Culture and the Phenomenon of Partial Reform', MIT, October 2003, to be published in Edward S. Steinfeld, *China's Market Visions*, forthcoming

p. 49   **when the Sun rises** 'The (Internally) Collected Quotations Of Chen Liangyu', http://chinadigitaltimes.net, September 2006

p. 49   **blueprint for a 'Harmonious Society'** Barry Naughton, 'The New Common Economic Program: China's 11th Five Year Plan and What It Means', Stanford University, Hoover Institution, *China Leadership Monitor,* no. 16 (Fall 2005)

Chapter Two

p. 56   **introduction of elections** Shuna Wang and Yang Yao, 'Grassroots Democracy and Local Governance: Evidence from Rural China', unpublished paper, February 2006; Yan Shen and Yang Yao, 'Grassroots Democracy and Income Distribution: Evidence from Village Elections in China', unpublished paper, April 2006

p. 70   **It harks back** James Fishkin, He Baogang, Alice Siu, 'Public Consultation in China: the First Chinese Deliberative Poll', unpublished paper, 2005

p. 71   **it shows how governments** Ibid.

p. 72 **have grown ten-fold** C. Fred Bergsten, Bates Gill, Nicholas R. Lardy and Derek Mitchell, *China: The Balance Sheet: What the World Needs to Know about the Emerging Superpower* (New York: PublicAffairs Books, 2007)

p. 73 **there were seventeen** Ibid.

p. 73 **had their lands confiscated** Ibid.

p. 73 **a further 2 million people** Ibid.

p. 77 **made no change at all** Wang Shaoguang, 'Patterns of China's public policy agenda setting', China Social Sciences issue 5 2006 (translated by Zhang Feng)

Chapter Three

p. 83 **The Rise of China** Yan Xuetong, 'The Rise of China in Chinese Eyes', *Journal of Contemporary China*, 10 (26) (2001), 33–44

p. 85 **the comprehensive power** Yan Xuetong, 'The Rise of China in Chinese Eyes', *Journal of Contemporary China*, 10 (26) (2001), 33–44

p. 87 **Deng Xiaoping meant** This was later developed into the twenty-four character strategy: 'Observe calmly; secure our position; cope with affairs calmly; hide our capacities and bide our time; be good at maintaining a low profile; and never claim leadership.'

p. 89 **China will not take** Zheng Bijian, *Peaceful Rise – China's New Road to Development* (Beijing: Central Party School Publishing House, 2005)

p. 91 **bloodless, less agressive** Wang Jisi, 'Peaceful Rise: A Discourse on China', 2006. Unpublished lecture, London School of Economics, 8 May 2006

p. 92 **In later speeches** Zheng Bijian, *Peaceful Rise – China's New Road to Development* (Beijing: Central Party School Publishing House, 2005)

p. 93   **the United State has** Yang Yi, 'Occupying the Moral Height of Enriching our Country and Empowering our Military', *Global Times*, 27 April 2006 (translated by Zhang Feng)

p. 95   **it has already set up** Tim Johnson, 'As China Rises, Many Rush to Get on Middle Kingdom Bandwagon', *San Jose Mercury News*, 25 October 2005

p. 95   **It has opened its universities** Joshua Kurlantzick, 'Responding to China's Charm Offensive', *Foreign Policy in Focus Commentary*, www.fpif.org

p. 96   **What we may be witnessing** Francis Fukuyama, 'The End of History?', *The National Interest*, Summer 1989

p. 97   **may even forge** Yan Xuetong, 'The Rise of China and its Power Status', *Chinese Journal of International Politics*, Vol. 1, 2006

p. 98   **A recent BBC World Service poll** 'China's influence seen positive' www.bbc.co.uk, 5 March 2005

p. 98   **If you do not have** Tim Johnson, 'China Rising: China's Global Influence Grows in Diplomacy, Trade, Culture', Knight Ridder Newspapers, 26 October 2005

p. 99   **a new organizing principle** 'Cooperative security is cheaper, more secure, scholars say' Stanford University News Service, 8 April 1992

p. 103 **To sustain its special relationship** Yan Xuetong, 'The Rise of China and its Power Status', *Chinese Journal of International Politics*, Vol. 1, 2006

p. 104 **Once [China] joined** Qin Yaqing and Wei Ling, 'Structures, Processes and the Socialization of Power: East Asian Community Building and the Rise of China', unpublished paper, 2006

p. 104 **if China had opposed** Ibid.

p. 104 **In an article** Yang Yi, 'Occupying the Moral Height of

Enriching our Country and Empowering our Military',
Global Times, 27 April 2006 (translated by Zhang Feng)

p. 107 **Economic prosperity** Qiao Liang and Wang Xiangsu,
Unrestricted Warfare (Beijing: PLA Literature and Arts
Publishing House, 1999)

p. 107 **it often makes** Ibid.

p. 108 **there are far-sighted** Ibid.

Conclusion

p. 116 **How can we** Wang Yiwei, 'Preventing the U.S. from
Declining Too Rapidly', *Global Times*, 10 August 2006
(translated by Zhang Feng)

p. 116 **shape an America** Shen Dingli, *Global Times*, 19
December 2005 (translated by Zhang Feng)

p. 116 **over the coming years** 'How China Runs the World
Economy', *The Economist*, 28 July 2005

p. 119 **even Africa's** Martin Davies, 'Special Economic Zones
and Infrastructure Corridors: China's Development
Model Comes to Africa', Stellenbosch University,
unpublished paper, May 2007

p. 120 **These governments** Jeffrey Sachs, 'The IMF and the Asian
Flu', *American Prospect*, 9 (March 1998)

p. 120 **This tale has been repeated** Chris Alden, 'Leveraging the
Dragon: Toward an Africa that Can Say No', *YaleGlobal
Online*, 1 March 2005, http://yaleglobal.yale.edu

p. 122 **The Chinese government** Andrew Leonard, 'No
Consensus on the Beijing Consensus: Neoliberalism with
Chinese Characteristics? Or the Long-Lost Third Way',
www.salon.com

p. 124 **coined the term** Arch Paddington, 'Freedom in the World
2007: freedom stagnation amid pushback democracy'
(Washington DC: Freedom House 2007)

p. 124 **a 'chilling effect'** Carl Gershman, 'The Backlash Against Democracy Assistance', testimony to the Committee on Foreign Relations of the United State Senate', 8 June 2007

p. 124 **Leading writers about democracy** Thomas Carothers, 'The Backlash Against Democracy Promotion,' Foreign Affairs, March/April 2006

p. 125 **China's growing foreign aid** Kenneth Roth, 'Filling the Leadership Void: Where is the European Union?' (New York: Human Rights Watch, 2007)

p. 126 **China also supplies** *Report to Congress of US-China Economic and Security Review Commission* (2006), http/www.uscc.gov

p. 126 **this is likely to involve** Larry Jagan, 'Myanmar Best Bad Buddies with Beijing', *Asia Times*, 13 June 2007

p. 127 **Acts of genocide** Tony Blair, 'Doctrine of the International Community,' speech at the Economic Club Chicago, 24 April 1999

p. 127 **Beijing is under pressure** 'Chinese Oil Investments in Sudan Hit US$6bn', *The Herald*, Khartoum, 27 June 2007

p. 129 **the United States was** Susan Shirk, 'China's Multilateral Diplomacy in the Asia-Pacific', evidence to the United States-China Economic and Security Review Commission, February 12–13 2004

p. 130 **On human rights** Richard Gowan, 'A Power of Audit of the United Nations' (London: European Council on Foreign Relations, forthcoming)

p. 130 **a paradigm shift** James Traub, 'The World According to China', *New York Times*, 3 September 2006

p. 131 **almost half the leaders** Lau Nai-keung, 'China Takes Its Place on the International Stage', *China Daily*, 30 December 2006

INDEX

MARK LEONARD is Executive Director of the European Council on Foreign Relations, the first pan-European think tank with offices in Berlin, London, Paris, Rome, Sofia and Warsaw. Previously he worked at the Centre for European Reform and was founding director of the Foreign Policy Centre. He has spent time in Washington as a Transatlantic fellow at the German Marshall Fund of the United States, and in Beijing as a visiting scholar at the Chinese Academy for Social Sciences. His first book, *Why Europe Will Run the 21st Century*, has been translated into 18 languages. Mark's essays and articles have appeared in publications on both sides of the Atlantic including *The Economist, The Guardian, The Financial Times, The Spectator, The Sun, Libération, Die Welt* and *The Wall Street Journal.*

www.markleonard.net

4+ż 4/09